Supplies

Also by Julia Cameron

nonfiction

The Artist's Way

The Artist's Way Morning Pages Journal

The Artist's Date Book
(illustrated by Elizabeth "Libby" Cameron)

The Vein of Gold

The Right to Write

God Is No Laughing Matter

God Is Dog Spelled Backwards
(illustrated by Elizabeth "Libby" Cameron)

Heart Steps

Blessings

Transitions

The Artist's Way at Work
(with Mark Bryan and Catherine Allen)

Money Drunk, Money Sober
(with Mark Bryan)

fiction

The Dark Room

Popcorn: Hollywood Stories

plays

Public Lives

The Animal in the Trees

Four Roses

Love in the DMZ

Avalon (*a musical*)

The Medium at Large (*a musical*)

poetry

Prayers for the Little Ones

Prayers for the Nature Spirits

The Quiet Animal

This Earth (*also an album with Tim Wheater*)

feature film

God's Will

A Pilot's Guide
to
Creative Flight

jeremy p. tarcher / putnam
a member of penguin putnam inc.
new york

Supplies

Julia Cameron

Illustrated by

Elizabeth Cameron

Most Tarcher/Putnam books are available at special quantity discounts for bulk purchase for sales promotions, premiums, fund-raising, and educational needs. Special books or book excerpts also can be created to fit specific needs. For details, write Putnam Special Markets, 375 Hudson Street, New York, NY 10014.

Jeremy P. Tarcher/Putnam

a member of

Penguin Putnam Inc.

375 Hudson Street

New York, NY 10014

www.penguinputnam.com

Library of Congress Cataloging-in-Publication Data

Cameron, Julia

    Supplies : A pilot's guide to creative flight / by Julia Cameron

      p. cm.

    ISBN 1-58542-066-2

      1. Creative ability—Problems, exercises, etc.   2. Self-actualizati

    (Psychology)—Problems, exercises, etc.   3. Creation (Literary,

    artistic, etc.) I. Title.

BF408.C176   2000   00-041810

153.3'5—dc21

Printed in the United States of America

10 9 8 7 6 5 4 3 2 1

This book is printed on acid-free paper. ∞

Book design by Deborah Kerner and Claire Vaccaro

Acknowledgements

For our spiritual mentors John Newland, Julianna McCarthy, Larry Lonergan, Max Showalter, Elberta Hornstein, Karen Johnson Boyd, Gini Buhler, and Fred M. Young, Sr.

For our family, especially our beloved aunts Bernice Murphy, Helen Harney, and Julie Rose Haas, and Julia's daughter, Domenica Cameron Scorsese.

And for our friends Joel Fotinos, Emma Lively, Susan Schulman, Jeremy Tarcher, Sonia Choquette, Martha Hamilton Snyder, Ilsa Hilbert Bruner, Nikki Keland, Sue Jensen, Claire Vaccaro and Sara Carder.

Introduction

Creativity is an act of initiative. It affects not only our physical but our psychic world. When we initiate a creative endeavor, we trigger the emergence of what might be called creative archetypes and experiences. Identifiable figures step forward to challenge our creative trajectory. These figures, experiences, and the stratagems for dealing with them form the content of this book.

Our creativity may be expressed in many areas—writing, painting, filmmaking, music—entrepreneurial enterprises of all stripes. The archetypes triggered remain constant, arena to arena. The successful facing down of these psychic dreadnaughts characterizes the inner accomplishment of successful creators. Once these internal and external characters are accurately identified and demystified, they can be dealt with on a humorous and preemptive level that siphons off their poisonous potency in our psyches.

"Non illegitimi te carborundum" is the rallying call for creative conquest: Don't let the bastards get you down.

The Arrow of Desire

Whenever we try to make or do something, we fire the Arrow of Desire. (It later turns into an airplane, but it starts as an arrow.) The Arrow of Desire knows exactly how to hit the bull's-eye, even if we think we can't or we don't. The trick with the arrow is to just aim and shoot. The trick can be tricky. You can't stop to think about it. You just have to do it. Commit.

Shoot the arrow. This isn't a NASA space shot, it's just a goddamn arrow, so shoot it. When you do that, you hit the bull's-eye. Commitment triggers support.

We often make the mistake of thinking we have to know how to do something instead of thinking that we *are* going to do something. Intention creates direction. The *what* dictates the *how*.

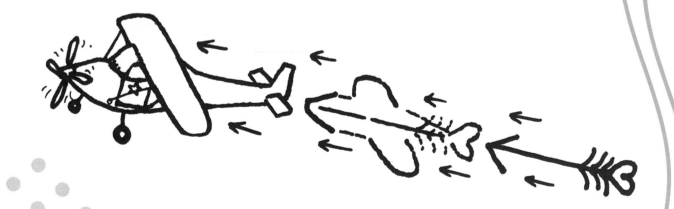

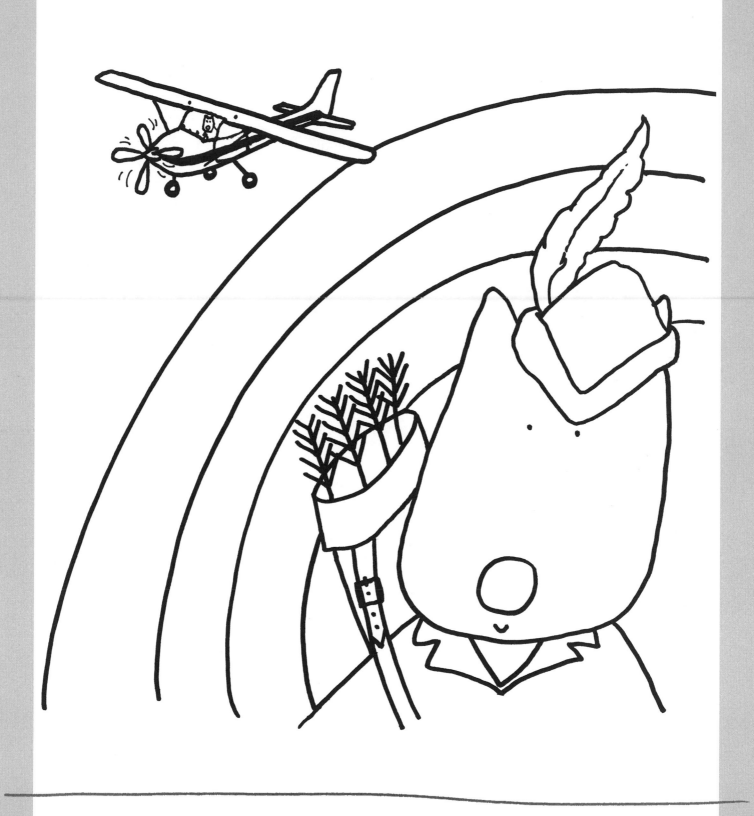

1   What do you desire to make?

2   Is this what you feel you *should* desire, or what you really *do* desire?

3   What *one* step could you take instantly to act on this desire?

4   Take that step.

5   Collect 10 magazines and pull images relating to your desired goal. Collage yourself at the height of your accomplished goal, using pictures of yourself and images that convey your dream and its successful fruition.

The Trickster Behind the Bull's-Eye

Lots of times when you are just about to fire the Arrow of Desire, a Trickster pops out from behind the bull's-eye and holds up a fake bull's-eye. Just a little to the side of the one you knew you wanted. The Trickster says, "Shoot at this instead." If you get fooled by the Trickster and shoot at his bull's-eye, you miss your own. It works like this.

The Trickster is a lot like Satan. He tempts you away from your heart and into your ego. He promises that if you do things his way, you'll get rich or famous or some other supposedly wonderful thing that's a little different from happy, which is what you get if you fire your own arrow at your own bull's-eye. (And if you do, you may also get rich and famous almost by accident.)

When you shoot your arrow, you can't think about stuff like rich and famous. You can't even take time out (like I've sometimes done) to argue with the Trickster about how you're right and he's wrong. When you are arguing, you are not firing the arrow, remember?

Sometimes, if you are shooting at a really big bull's-eye, with a really great Arrow of Desire, all sorts of Tricksters will pop out. It's almost like the dance of the seven veils. There's a Tarot card about this one, the Seven of Cups, I think. You're just about to fire the arrow and suddenly there're nine thousand diverting, seductive things all wiggling their ass at you.

You know how this goes. Or how it can go.

You're about to get happily married and somehow you have a torrid one-night stand with Miss Poison, your fiancée's evil best friend.

You're about to take the new job you want when your Terrible Boss offers you more money than God.

You're about to gallop off into the sunset with your own dream, when the Damsel in Distress tempts you to get off your horse and rescue her and *her* dream.

Or you're a girl with her own white horse and you're just leaping the fence to freedom, when you see this very handsome wounded warrior who could use your help. . . .

You get the picture. I hate this picture. So I've learned that sometimes you just have to close your eyes, aim with your heart, and shoot.

A ditty:

LISTEN TO YOUR HEART STEPS AND FOLLOW WHERE THEY LEAD.

AN EAR FOR YOUR OWN MUSIC WILL TEACH YOU ALL YOU NEED.

THE LISTENING HEART IS WHERE TO START, IT'S THERE YOU GET YOUR START.

THE ARROW OF DESIRE HITS THE BULL'S-EYE LIKE A DART.

1   Have you ever encountered the Trickster behind the bull's-eye?

2   What false goal did you pursue as a result?

3   What false goal can still trick you?

4   Do you have a repeat offender Trickster in your life?

5   Who helps you aim truly?

The Shadow Maker

I believe each of us is like a little airplane with a device built in that I call The Shadow Maker. The device is there to tell you how high you can fly safely. You get to a certain height and the device flips on and it makes big scary shadows when you look down, and the higher you go, the worse the shadows get and so usually you hurry up and head back down and land.

In a way, the Shadow Maker can be a good thing because it keeps you from flying straight into the stratosphere. On the other hand, a lot of us have our Shadow Makers set at too low an altitude so that we abort our flights when actually we have a lot more safe air space left. The height our Shadow Maker is set at determines our creative ceiling.

It's a lot like in the movie *The Right Stuff*, where the sound barrier was everybody's ceiling until Sam Shepard, I mean Chuck Yeager, came along and he didn't believe in it the same way. His Shadow Maker was set beyond the sound barrier so he sailed right through it. After he did it, a lot of other people did and we've pretty much been doing it ever since.

Our Shadow Makers get set at their altitude by a lot of different people and a lot of little things. Your mom might set it low, or your dad. Your childhood religion might set it low. Or your spouse. Or a jealous teacher. They set it low for a lot of reasons and often it's their own fear or jealousy that tells them where they think they ought to set your creative ceiling. It's a lot like having an airplane worked on by too many mechanics who may or may not know your particular machine.

Once you know you've got a Shadow Maker, you can begin to think about whether or not it's set at the right height for you. (Usually, it's not. Usually, it's too low.) You can begin to experiment with nudging it higher, and when it flicks on, say to yourself, "Oh, there it goes, the Shadow Maker." A few people have Shadow Makers set too high, but the odds are good you aren't one of them. I'd say one in a thousand, maybe. One in ten thousand. Most of us ask the wrong question, "Too high and grandiose?" when we should really be asking, "Too low?"

1   What triggers your Shadow Maker?

2   Who installed your Shadow Maker?

3   Who thinks you're too big for your britches?

4   Do you sabotage your flight when your Shadow Maker is activated?

5   Who helps you set your Shadow Maker higher?

13

Strobe Light Clarity

Creative breakthroughs are often accompanied by something I call Strobe Light Clarity. Just for a second, the light—or the lightning—flashes and you see the landscape clearly but with exaggerated shadows, your own and everyone else's. Everything looks very black and white. "She's using me," you decide, or "see" about an old friend and you're right about that. What you are not right about is the harshness of the situation. There were more grays to the picture than you see in your first flash. On the other hand, you are not wrong about what you saw.

Strobe Light Clarity is how we break the code on something. It's what happens when we get the lay of the land, but all it tells us are the harsh cartoon outlines, not the details.

Strobe Light Clarity can be very useful and very scary. It's what happens when our denial breaks. One of the roughest parts about Strobe Light Clarity is that it comes and goes, as the name suggests. You see the picture and then you don't. You get pitched back and forth between clarity and doubt: I saw it. I think I saw it. I see it. I don't see it.

There's a famous drawing used in psychological tests that shows either a face or a vase, depending on how you look at it. That's what Strobe Light Clarity does with reality. It shows you a new way of looking at something. It reverses figure and ground.

When you are having Strobe Light Clarity, you are walking in tricky terrain. You can be both dazzled and blinded by what you see. The lighting is so severe that it's hard to get perspective. Strobe Light Clarity

is a heightened and exaggerated reality. It is based on the true shape of things, but it can also be misleading. Sometimes it's best just to know what you saw, not deny it, but not act on it either.

1   Have you ever experienced Strobe Light Clarity?

2   What did you "suddenly" see?

3   Have you learned to identify restlessness, anger, and frustration as the early warning signals of a breakthrough?

4   What do you feel you are about to see clearly?

5   Whom can you trust to reinforce and help you hold your new clarity?

The Identified Patient Voice

One of the things that happens when you start to see things clearly is that those who've got a vested interest in keeping you fuzzy will start to act like you're going crazy. Even if they can behave reasonably well most of the time and hide their agendas and smile and be nice, the minute you start to change the rules, the gloves are off and here's what happens. They get out their Identified Patient Voice, the one they used on Frances Farmer and, for that matter, on Galileo, right before they threw him out of the church for saying the world was round.

If you ever had a moment of clarity around someone who didn't want you to, you've probably heard the Voice. It's sort of fakey sweet and soothing and it's usually slowed down a little, like maybe you're a little dumb. It's also very solemn because if anyone cracks a joke or laughs at a moment like this, the game's up and they may not be able to get you into the straitjacket after all.

The Voice they use goes, "Mmmm, yes, well, that's very interesting." They act like you've just said UFOs had landed on the roof like reindeer (which maybe they had).

The Identified Patient Voice they use means you are the crazy one and they are the Identified Loving Caretaker. You're nuts. They're sane. Those are the rules, and it's not funny.

Let's say your lover is having an affair and you know it because you found somebody else's red bikini pants in your bed after you came home from a business trip. Let's say you even know whose bikini pants they might be. Let's say you even have mental Polaroids of the whole

DO NOT BE FOOLED.
THOSE ARE GWEN'S UNDERPANTS.

setup. You say, "You're having an affair with Gwen!"

Out comes the Voice. "I'm sorry you feel that way. It must be hard being so insecure. Did you get enough sleep on your trip? You're under a lot of stress. Those underpants probably just got messed up with our stuff at the laundry."

Plausible. Possible. Not true. Don't be fooled. Those *are* Gwen's underpants.

Let's say somebody at work has been presenting your ideas as his own. Just say so and out comes the Voice, "Gee, Jean, I'm sorry you feel like that. You know corporate life is really a collaborative process and if you're threatened by that, maybe you should try to process it a little with your shrink or the counselor in Employee Relationships. I can tell you're feeling a little fragile, so I'll see if I can put in for some vacation time for you. . . ."

What do you say, "Okay, Brutus"?

I've said, "Okay, Brutus," a lot and that's how I've learned it is the Wrong Thing to Do. It's better to go into the bathroom and recite, "I'm not crazy, I'm not crazy. I'm not crazy," even if then you really sound crazy.

You are not.

1   Have you ever heard the Identified Patient Voice?

2   When have you been treated like you were crazy, when really you were right?

3   Who in your life can convince you you're crazy and use that to their advantage?

4   Can you identify and discount the Identified Patient Voice when you hear it?

5   Have you learned that hearing this Voice may mean you are on the *right* track?

Monster in the Mirror

Another thing that happens when you start to have a breakthrough is that sometimes you see the Monster in the Mirror. The Monster in the Mirror is the Worst Possible Thing You Could Be. It's kind of like you're this wonderful zippy little airplane flying along and then you look down and see your shadow and it looks like you might be some dark and evil hideous bird of prey but you didn't know it. It's like you've suddenly stumbled into a Disney movie and you're the Wicked Witch.

The Monster in the Mirror can be triggered by almost any good-for-you change. (And sometimes the people around you like to make you think you're the Monster in the Mirror, because then they don't have to change.) Monster in the Mirror is half your distorted perception and half the scary voice-over others use.

"Pick up your clothes," you say. "Or—here's a new idea—you can't go to the movies." Presto: Monster in the Mirror.

"Mom, I would pick them up, but I think I'm getting an ear infection or something. I feel kind of dizzy like I might be getting a fever, and you've been so busy (unfit mother) I don't want to worry you. . . ." Oh, yes they do. Bad Mommy, shame, shame, poor little Cinderella kid. And, of course, they might really have an ear infection, but still, don't get confused.

Anytime you ask somebody to be a little more accountable, they might flash you the Monster in the Mirror.

"Your child support check bounced."

"You mean you cashed it?!" (Greedy ex-wife, money-grubber, naughty, naughty . . .)

The Monster in the Mirror says really fun things. Like on this book I am getting "Since you're funny and Harry Potter is funny and you mention Harry Potter, everybody will say that you stole your funniness from Harry Potter." (No, but I do channel him every Friday night.)

The Monster in the Mirror will say whatever mean and horrible thing it can think of to keep you from changing. Or from doing anything fun.

Jungians sometimes call the Monster in the Mirror the "Shadow." Why only one shadow? I see lots of them when the Monster is around! They also call it the "animus," as in animosity, I guess. Make no mistake, the Monster in the Mirror speaks pure venom. "Who do you think you are?" it hisses, and then it tries to tell you.

Let's say you do something nice for someone. The Monster in the Mirror will tell you that it's actually a covert attempt to control them.

THE BEST THING YOU CAN DO WITH THE MONSTER IN THE MIRROR IS STICK YOUR TONGUE OUT AT IT.

The Monster in the Mirror likes to keep you looking in the Mirror, examining you and your motives like you've got a bad spiritual complexion. If it can keep you picking at yourself, it can probably keep you from doing anything.

The best thing to do with the Monster in the Mirror is to stick your tongue out at it. The Monster in the Mirror hates to be laughed at. Laughter makes it vanish. My friend Sonia Choquette says that "laughter chases Satan away."

Maybe the Monster in the Mirror *is* Satan—although the Monster will say you are.

Flash it the bird.

1 Have you ever encountered the Monster-in-the-Mirror phenomenon?

2 Are you struck down by it often, seldom, never?

3 What triggers its cruelty?

4 What's the worst thing it has ever said to you?

5 What action do you take to antidote the poison?

The Grand Canyon of Doubt

Changing a size to a bigger one actually feels like an acid trip or one of those scary adventures that Castañeda had with Don Peyote, or whatever his name was. Here's what I mean. You decide to take some risk and it looks okay, like you can do it. Like you're a little kid running across a field and going to jump a tiny little creek the size of a wriggly worm. Okay, you start running toward the risk (new job, marriage, baby, publishing your little book) and all of a sudden you look up and the tiny little creek has turned into the Grand Canyon, and if you try to leap it you're going to die, die, die!

What do you do? Stop running? Lose your momentum so you fall on your face in the creek? That will happen if you listen to your doubts. The trick is to speed up and jump! After that it's just a little creek, except for those few horrible moments midair when you know it's the Grand Canyon—and that you are this tiny little amphetamined ant trying to jump something *huge*!

You are not a tiny little demented ant. Jump!

REMOVE BEFORE FLIGHT

THE TRICK IS TO SPEED UP AND JUMP.

1 What creative jump looms large to you?

2 What can you do to pick up your attitude and momentum to clear it?

3 Whom can you enlist as booster rockets to help you make the jump?

4 Have you thought of asking for prayers for your creative projects?

5 How can you celebrate having made the jump?

Alice in Wonderland

One of the things that happens whenever you are growing bigger is that you start changing sizes like crazy. In the long run you'll end up bigger, but when you're growing you'll be big and then small, big and then small, big and then small. Eventually, you'll come back together bigger, but for a while you'll be tiny like an ant or like that giant Mr. Puffy walking through the streets in *Ghostbusters*.

Shrinks would say you are trying to "integrate." I'd say, "stabilize."

1 At your very largest, who are you?

2 At your very smallest, who do you fear you are?

3 In the eyes of your most supportive friend, who are you?

4 Write out a description of yourself at your very best.

5 Buy or make a "God Jar," a beautiful container in which you place your dreams for incubation. Place your description of yourself in the jar.

The Fun House

A lot of us grew up in the Fun House. You know what happens in the Fun House (Orson Welles put it in *The Lady From Shanghai*, if you don't). In the Fun House, when you look in the mirror to get a reflection you don't look like who you are at all. You look like a fat little cartoon dwarf. You look like a tall, skinny skeleton. Your face has weird angles. Your body has weird lumps. (Like the kind of mirrors you run into when you try to buy a bathing suit, but worse.)

Growing up in the Fun House means you don't get a lot of accurate information about who you are or what you might be able to do. You're like poor orphan Harry Potter growing up with the Muggles and not knowing you're a wizard. You get reflected back to yourself as too big for your britches or else too little to fill your shoes, the ones you're trying to step into.

You get conversations like this:

"I think I'd like to be a writer (or anything else fun)."

"Don't you think you might need something to fall back on?"

In the Fun House, you never get it together to answer "No, actually, I think I'll make a fortune doing what I want because I love it and I'll be good at it."

In the Fun House, they hand out Shrink-You pills whenever you get uppity. (Sometimes they hand out actual shrinks as well.)

It's bad enough growing up in the Fun House, but sometimes because it's the habitat we're used to, we build the Fun House again when we grow up. Instead of filling our lives with Believing Mirrors, which reflect us back as gifted and competent, we fill our lives with the familiar old Fun House Mirrors. We get wives and husbands who hand us Shrink-

You pills. They have our second and third and fourth thoughts for us in case we're not already scared and having them ourselves. It goes like this:

"I think I want to change jobs!"

"Oh, honey, are you sure you should? I mean, you've got a lot of security and you're close to retirement age in another fifty years and you even know how to drive there. . . ."

No, they don't actually say that, but almost.

If you talk to a Fun House Mirror or look in its face to see how you are doing, what you see is Worry . . . Concern . . . and maybe this little slogan floating over your head that says, "Think Smaller."

Don't.

1   Did you grow up in the Fun House?

2   Who were your Distorting Mirrors, distorting your sense of identity?

3   Who were your Believing Mirrors, mirroring your potential?

4   Did your school or religion function as a Fun House for you?

5   When you step into a Fun House dynamic, can you identify and discount it?

Wet-Blanket Matadors

A lot of people get scared when you get smart. It's like they've got all their Sacred Cows carefully rounded up in their mental corral and they are afraid you're going to turn them loose and then they'll get trampled to death by New Thoughts and New Perspectives, dangerous things that might catch them on the horns and pierce their denial or their serious hot air balloon or something dreadful.

Let's say you're charging ahead like a bull with some fabulous idea that's hilarious and brilliant. Better watch out. Out will come the Wet-Blanket Matadors. They use their Wet-Blanket energy to baffle and confuse you like the poor bull, so you end up on the ground bleeding and stuck full of swords.

You run into a lot of Wet-Blanket Matadors in business meetings and committee meetings. Although they'd deny it, they are total control freaks and when you bring some great bullish new idea into the room, they really freak out. They grab for the Wet Blanket and wave it in front of your face in order to deflect you because your charge forward has scared them silly. They start shrieking things like: "I've got a little problem with that idea, Josh," and then they wave the Big Wet Blanket of seriousness. If they're any good at this, pretty soon they can get the whole room doing it, playing the Wet Blanket Here's Why We Can't Do It game.

"It's the money!" (Stab!)

"It's the time!" (Stab!)

"It's not done that way!" (Stab!)

"There are the rules to think of!" (Stab!)

Pretty soon, there you are in the middle of the meeting, bleeding like the poor bull, down on your knees and dying of embarrassment because you were dumb enough to try to be smart. And some of these Wet-Blanket Matadors are really mean. They get into it like your corporate death is Brutus stabbing Julius Caesar. (Actually, I like the Matador idea better. The Caesar idea sounds like a lot of bull.)

YOU RUN INTO A LOT OF WET BLANKET MATADORS IN BUSINESS MEETINGS AND COMMITTEE MEETINGS.

1   Have you ever encountered a
    Wet-Blanket Matador?

2   Do you know of any repeat offenders?

3   How are your ideas most frequently
    Wet Blanketed?

4   What's your Achilles' heel in terms of shaking
    your self-confidence?

5   What stratagem can you use to disarm
    the Wet-Blanket Matadors in your life?

Shrinks

Okay. I think there is a reason we call them Shrinks. It's because that's what the bad ones can do to you. They can shrink you until you're so small that you can't do anything without talking to them about it. Because they're big and strong and you've been, well, shrunk.

Now, not all Shrinks do this. Some Shrinks actually help you to shrink your problems. Those are the good Shrinks, but they're hard to find, maybe because they shrink or something and you have to search really hard to find them.

So, Shrinks are a tricky thing because sometimes they don't shrink. They shrink you while they grow huge (this trick is called projection) and supposedly it's your fault and you do it to them, but actually I think a lot of Shrinks are complicitous in this little trick.

You say, "I don't think you're hearing me properly," and they say, "Do you have a problem—maybe with your *father* not hearing you properly?"

That's a scary thought, and it makes it hard to be able to say, "Actually, Dad seemed to listen pretty well, it's you I'm talking about."

Sometimes if you say that you don't like something about what they are doing, they will say, "Let's process that for a while." What this really means, although they are trying to disguise it, is "I am not willing to hear or honor your perception and this is a great opportunity to do what I am secretly dying to do, which is to make your session, the one you're paying for, about me, your Shrink, or at least about us, so that I get a part somewhere in here."

You've got to be really careful about Shrinks and creativity. Usually they can't admit that it might just be fun to do things. They want you to think about how you might be compensating. Or how it's a neurotic defense mechanism or an attempt to shore up a rickety ego or, or, or . . . Shrinks can be very creative about helping people not be creative. Shrinks don't like the "just do it" part. They like the more expensive, "Let's talk about why you want to do it or not do it" part.

Most Shrinks should be shrunk. We've already got a perfectly good God, and they should remember that.

SHRINKS ARE A TRICKY THING BECAUSE SOMETIMES THEY DON'T SHRINK.

THEY SHRINK YOU WHILE THEY GROW HUGE.

1 Have you ever been shrunk by a Shrink?

2 In what ways were you miniaturized or diminished?

3 Have you ever been enlarged by a Shrink?

4 In what ways were you supported and encouraged?

5 Do you respect your creativity as a healthy urge?

Very Serious People

First cousins to Shrinks are another batch of trouble I call Very Serious People. They can drain the life out of you in a nanosecond. As a rule, you start to attract them in droves the minute you start to lighten up and have fun. Or maybe they've always been in your life, but you suddenly really notice them, the way an annoying clock sounds if the house gets quiet.

Very Serious People *are* a lot like clocks. Or maybe like bombs. They like to keep tick-tick-ticking no matter what. Be as funny as you want. As zany as monkeys in hula skirts, and they will not smile. They like to say sort of thin-lipped things like "Your dog is barking" when an exuberant puppy is snuffling around and yipping and trying to kiss them in excitement. If you get excited, they do the same thing to you: "Get down, Rover!"

Very Serious People like to talk about very serious things like war and famine and the neighborhood getting wrecked by *them*. As a rule, they pretty much agree that the world is a terrible place and we can't do much about it and they like to explain the fine points of why. God help you if you raise a festive or creative idea in their midst.

"This is serious," they snap, like you've just begged for food from the table. Sometimes when I am around Very Serious People, I think my name should be Bad Julie. Just like Bad Rover, Bad Julie tends to get excited and want to have fun and this is not their idea of fun, not at all. Their idea of fun is being serious.

Serious people are a lot like bad therapists. They are really good at doing "Isn't it tragic the way we have all been wounded?" And, just like bad therapists, they tend to get stuck there. You can imagine what this can do to a dinner party. It's like playing Pachelbel's Canon when you could also play the Beatles.

Very Serious People have very serious ideas about almost everything. Especially about things like Serious Art and Serious Artist. They like to talk about Orson and Ernest and they're a lot more Ernest than Ernest ever was when they do it.

Of course, when people are talking about Masters and Masterpieces all the time instead of about what they're actually doing or about what you're actually doing, in other words, when they are stuck in theory and not in doing things, you and your bright idea can be made to look pretty dim. They have a special patented withering glance that they use to dim the radiance of anybody who gets a little festive around them.

Very Serious People tend to be pretty vague or even snappish when you ask them a direct question about their actual life. Maybe it seems like small talk to them compared to Orson's or Elia's lives. Certainly compared to Ken Wilbur's.

I sometimes wonder if Serious People take themselves so seriously because they don't really take themselves seriously at all. If they did, they just might lighten up.

1   Have you learned to distinguish the difference in energy between artists and intellectuals?

2   Does your life circle contain some Very Serious People?

3   What is the impact of their energies upon your own?

4   Have you learned that humor accelerates your creative energies?

5   Name five of your favorite comedies and rent one.

Very Important People

Another thing that can really take the wind out of you just as you're picking up steam is to run into a Very Important Person. I'm not talking about a Really Important Person, I mean the other kind, the kind that has to act important.

Very Important People can act an awful lot like Amateur Experts. They have the same bad habit of trying to ram how important they are down your throat or your ears—whichever is available.

I've always thought that in the movie business they should be called "Come on over and shake your head" meetings, because they seemed to be about seeing how big they were.

But I don't want to act like movie people have a lock on being Very Important People. (Lots of movie people are actually fun even when they are Really Important.) No, Very Important People are like social crabgrass. They turn up everywhere: New York, Chicago, Boston, Your Town.

Very Important People often drive very important cars and wear very important clothes and smell good or at least very important. They live at important addresses, shop at important stores, and travel with a little group of pilot fish so you will know they are important. Sometimes the pilot fish act even more important than the Big Fish. In fact, usually.

When you run into a Very Important Person you will notice that he or she is pretty confused. It's like they actually believe that acting important is the same as being important. They will say things like "Unless you drive the right car, nobody will take you seriously creatively."

I think that's hooey. People are smarter than that. As for me, I have always been crystal clear that our ideas are the Learjet, and I think when they get a grip, almost anybody would know the same thing.

Remember that ideas are the real toys and that you've got those. You're secretly independently wealthy. Enjoy the secret.

The trick when you meet a Very Important Person is not to get into it. Do not play, "I qualify for your club." You may have one tennis court, but somebody else will always have two. Try to think of that stuff as "toys." That makes it funnier and easier to take.

All the Very Important People who snub you today will eventually suck up to you if you make it, so don't bother trying to impress them now.

Travel light, and that means light-hearted.

1 Have you ever encountered Very Important People?

2 Do you recognize self-importance as a defense mechanism?

3 What status symbols speak to you the most loudly?

4 What status symbols would you never be caught dead with?

5 What status symbol would you secretly love to have?

Experts

I've probably got a short fuse—or maybe a big lack of humility, but I hate self-appointed Experts. I've noticed that when you try to talk to some people, it's like you just pushed the button marked PLAY. (And I don't mean on a teeter-totter.)

You try to talk to them, but all you've really done is activate their talk button. Right away they go into Expert mode and, without trying to figure out what you might already know about something—we're all pretty bright, it seems to me—they start trying to download absolutely everything they know, relevant or not, about the topic you brought up. It's like they think conversation is a game of Trivial Pursuit. And they are demon competitive. Conversationally, Amateur Experts are all over the court, playing every position.

I think it all boils down to they're not very interested in learning who you are. They're really more interested in telling you who they are. You're only "officially" talking. Really, you're supposed to be the audience.

I know some people who know an awful lot about everything. Just ask them. Worse yet, accidentally ask them. Tell them you want to buy lettuce and get the insecticide lecture. Tell them you want to go to the movies and get the How-the-Movie-Business-Has-Sold-Out lecture. Tell them you want a cup of coffee and get the caffeine lecture and the How-There-Was-the-Decaf-with-Bad-Chemicals lecture. With some people, it's like their whole life's job is to lecture. They were coming down the chute from heaven and God swatted them on their baby ass and said, "Okay, you, Henry, play Expert," and then sent them into the game.

It's a lot like basketball. You really ought to play the slot you're good at. Like if you want to play center and lecture, then you ought to make sure you're tall enough and you're not delivering your lecture to Magic Johnson or Michael Jordan. One of the things I have noticed about real Experts is that they don't seem to need to lecture all the time.

1 Have you ever listened to an Expert over your own intuition?

2 Have you ever let an Expert talk you out of a worthy risk?

3 Have you learned to think of Experts as service mechanics for your projects?

4 Do you realize that expertise *about* something is different from the ability to *do* something?

5 Are there Experts who you admire and find useful and inspiring?

How to Use the Telescope: Turn It Around

When it comes to our talents, telescopes are wonderful things. It's just that we keep holding them at the wrong end. (This is the way we have been taught to hold them by the Business.) So, let's start with Hollywood, but the game is played everywhere.

Let's say you're an actor. You get handed the backward telescope all the time. You go to an audition and there you all are like tiny little miniature gears in a huge and scary and impersonal machine. That's how you have been trained to look at it. Sitting in the holding area, you look at one another and there too you've got the telescope turned so that the others look big and competent and you look tiny and uncastable.

The game being played is "You are tiny and dispensable" and "Unless we tell you you can act, you have to wait around for years." Nonsense. You're the one with the talent. Act in your living room if you have to. Do it for fun and for love and whenever you can and remember you are the one with the power. Without actors they can't make movies, now, can they?

As a writer, they turn the telescope around by playing Expert and saying, "There are very few good scripts in this town." Nonsense. There are zillions of good scripts, even great scripts. The part that's missing isn't how to write them. It's how to read them. We used to joke that if you told a director "A bridge in the jungle," he saw what you did: the chasm, the vines, the rickety bridge with frayed rope, the water down below. Tell a studio executive and he sees the Ventura Freeway.

Okay, I am not being fair. A lot of studio people are blocked artists themselves and that's why they are so miserable. Everyone came here to make movies and not money, but we all forgot this.

I am not saying studio people are dumb. I'm just saying they've got the telescope backwards too. They do not use it to see what's good with a script and magnify those parts, which is how to say yes and make a movie. They use it to magnify what might be wrong and concentrate on how not to make a movie. And how to say no. (In their past lives, a lot of studio executives and publishing executives were shrinks and they are great at analyzing just what's wrong, but God forbid they make something.)

I don't want to make it sound like Hollywood is the only place the Telescope Game is played. They are great at it in New York publishing, too. This is why God made the Internet. (Yes, God made the Internet and God made cheap but good digital cameras so that people could get their work done. There's a reason God is called the Creator. He sides with the talent.)

If you look at Hollywood or publishing accurately, you see that it's like one of those movies where it's time for a revolution but the people don't know they have that power. Instead, they listen to the loudspeakers up on the tops of buildings that shout, "You there. Lowly writer! Who do you think you are?" Or "Actor worm, don't get uppity or it's solitary for you!"

The whole power system is precisely upside down, like a great big lovely gooey cake that's had its face mashed in the table. The deal is this: "Management" runs the game and "talent" is the slave class. No wonder people get neurotic and sleazy and manipulative sometimes. It goes with the territory of being a slave. It's what you think you have to do to skin the cat. When people say, "Artists are so neurotic," they might want to think about how neurotic they'd be if they were being miniaturized, discounted, dissed, and having the rug pulled out from under them all the time.

Back to the telescope.

We are taught to hold it so that when we look at agents and managers and studio people, they look big and scary. "My God, they're giant! They'll crush me and Toto," we think. (You can see where this is going.) One reason studio people

brag about their guns—I mean their big-shot salaries—and toys is so we won't notice they're the same size we are. Or maybe a little smaller. It's the Telescope Trick again.

If you think about the state of the arts as being a little like Rome before the collapse, you get the picture. Star artists are like the house slaves who get pampered. Money is used like a drug to keep writers and actors and directors and producers so drugged up with things that they don't notice they are the ones with the power and that they aren't often using it to make things.

I could be wrong about this, but I think we're on the brink of some major naughtiness. I've known a few directors and the truth is they like to direct—and all the time if they could. They like that more than the money and the jet and the treats they've been doped up with. Even the big directors are really happier when they are making movies. Even little movies. Which is exactly what I think they're going to be doing in about another minute.

Talent is like Gulliver and it's waking up. What are all the ropes? Who are all those tiny people trying to control me?

1 Who in your life miniaturizes your dreams?

2 Who in your life miniaturizes your talents?

3 Who in your life miniaturizes your problems?

4 Who in your life enlarges and expands your vision?

5 Who in your life enriches and extends your talents?

The Lug-Bolt Mentality

We're Americans. We invented the assembly line. We went along with the disastrous idea that it might be better to do one tiny little thing a million times a day than have the joy of making the whole gadget. This is why people like Fred at the plant in Detroit feel a little crazy. He goes around saying what the company tells him: "You make Ford!" but really Fred just gets to make a lug bolt, and he knows it.

Poor Fred. Poor us. We carry lug-bolt thinking everywhere, and it sure shows up in the arts. Now that the arts are a big machine, artists get to get stuck with lug-bolt thinking. If they make one thing well, they are supposed to keep right on making that. In movies, Scorsese is allowed to make gangster lug bolts, for example. And if he gets uppity and wants to do a different nut, the critics are standing there like factory managers to yell,

"Stick with the lug bolt, goddamm it, Marty!" Or "Stick with the extraterrestrials, naughty, bad Steven!"

A lot of times we worry about being "dilettantes" when actually what we should be worrying about is "Am I stuck in the lug-bolt slot?" Now, if you like doing the lug bolt, and you are satisfied, fine. Make a million lug bolts. But if you want to change, change. And don't listen to the people who say you shouldn't or you can't.

Try it and see how it works out. After you've done it seven or eight thousand times, even the critics might let you. They might say, "Gee, even better at this than the lug bolt. Keep at this one. Keep at this one."

For an artist, being stuck in the lug-bolt position is like being stuck in the missionary position—better than nothing, I suppose.

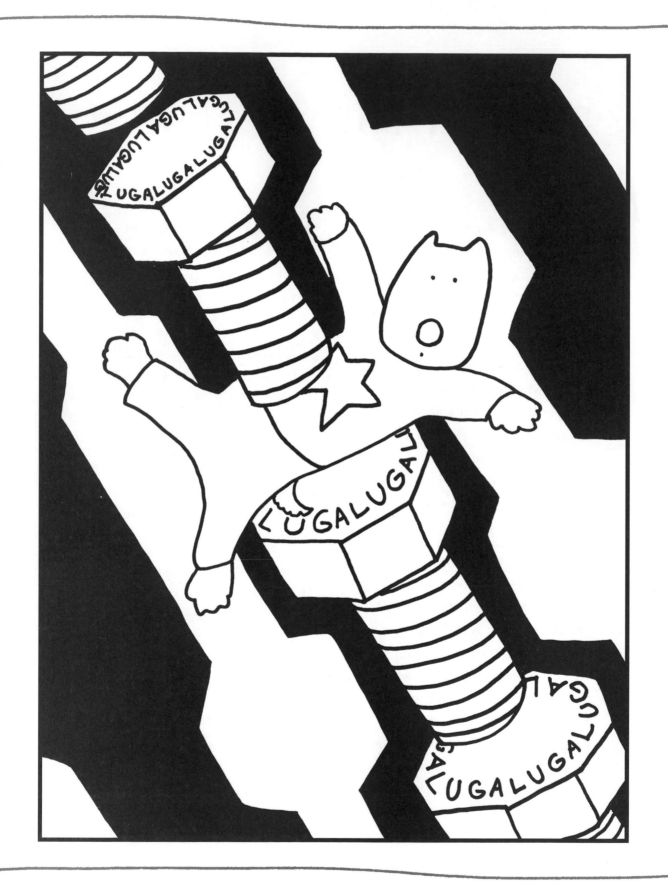

1   What lug bolt are you acknowledged for your skill at?

2   Does this lug bolt satisfy you?

3   In what way?

4   Is there another lug bolt you'd like to try your hand at?

5   What's preventing you from simply trying?

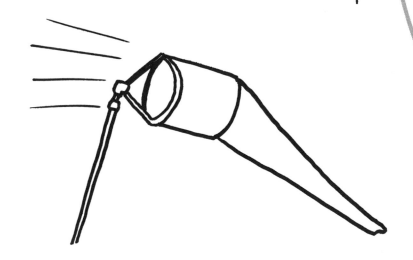

Fuse Lighters

There are people who can set us off like rockets. We meet them and we catch on fire. Ideas go off like firecrackers. We make a gorgeous display of fireworks. They spark us into sparkling. These people are our muses. Although it may feel like a torrid affair—and we sometimes do that too—what we really make with these people are our brainchildren. There's a reason we call them brain*children*. Sexual energy and creative energy both make love and babies.

I've married two of my muses and kept an electric arm's length from a few more. I've learned that even though it may feel like we're supposed to run off into the sunset together, we might really only be supposed to make songs not whoopee, movies not happy endings. (Although it's great when you can sometimes do both.)

It's my experience that some of us can do better with Fuse Lighters if we let them light the fuse and leave than if we grab them by the ankles and try to get them to stay. I've had encounters with muses that were like creative one-night stands where I got pregnant with a movie, musical, or book.

When you meet a Fuse Lighter, you build things. Sometimes it's a life together and sometimes it's a toy together. Fuse Lighters teach us that there are all kinds of true love, and when two people are Fuse Lighters for each other, it's a pretty big gift. I've had that a few times, and I wish it on everyone along with the proviso to try not to burn down the house.

1   Name five Fuse Lighters from your past and present.

2   What projects or dreams did they help you to ignite?

3   What have you done to thank them?

4   Who serves as a Fuse Lighter on your current projects?

5   For whom are you a Fuse Lighter?

REMOVE BEFORE FLIGHT

Booster Rockets

When you're revving up your engines and you're wondering if you've got enough power to make it into orbit, your Booster Rockets show up. Booster Rockets are people you feel a keen and quick kinship with. A sense of glad to see you. Not like "Oh, my God, true love." More like "Glad you finally showed up. Now let's get this show on the road."

When you meet a Booster Rocket, you feel brighter and clearer and cleaner. Maybe you eat dinner with them, and the next day, for no reason, you suddenly see what your next step should really be. Booster Rockets are not necessarily along for the whole ride. A lot of times after they're done doing what they do, they just sort of fall away. A lot of times they circle back years later when you're at a higher altitude and perform the exact same function again.

A lot of the time if someone is a Booster Rocket for you, you are the same for them. It doesn't feel like hauling each other up by the bootstraps, rescuing each other. It feels like "Here. Let me give that strap a yank." Quick, easy, done, and incredibly helpful.

1   Are you open enough to accept help?

2   What Booster Rockets have you combined with successfully?

3   Who among your friends boosts your energy as their own?

4   Is your significant other a Booster Rocket?

5   Are you a Booster Rocket to the working projects of others?

Piggybackers

The brighter and more heated up your creative furnace gets, the more you will start to attract two things: opportunities and Piggybackers. The opportunities, you want. The Piggybackers, you don't want.

It is absolutely true that success occurs in clusters and is born out of generosity. It is absolutely false that this means you should give freeloaders a free ride. Your true friends and supporters are the ones who row their own boat instead of trying to jump into yours. Your real friends and supporters bring something to the picnic instead of just showing up to gobble the goodies you've made. It may take a little practice, but you'll be able to tell the difference.

One thing you should be told about Piggybackers is that they like to present themselves as an opportunity for you. Since most of us are a little starved for opportunity and attention, we can get fooled by a bit of flattery about how great we are into thinking that what the Piggybacker is offering is a great opportunity.

Piggybackers are diversions. They don't really want to help you, they want you to help them. People on the verge of a breakthrough seem to give off a faint perfume that Piggybackers can smell a mile away. Suddenly, they're your best friend. They'd like to take you to lunch. They'd like to hear all about what you're doing. . . . Don't tell them. In fact, don't go to lunch even if they want to treat you to the best lunch in town; if you let the Piggybacker in, it can be an expensive meal in the long run.

Here's a little ditty a Piggybacker
might sing:

A CAPITAL INVESTMENT!
YOUR MODEST LITTLE PLAN
IS THE SORT OF BUILDING BLOCK
THAT MADE ME THE MAN I AM.

YOUR MUSTARD SEED'S A MIGHTY OAK
OR THE JOKE'S ON ME.
LET'S PLAY REAL AND MAKE A DEAL—
I'LL SIGN AND YOU CAN SEAL!

YOUR GENIUS FOR INVENTION,
THAT'S THE CARD YOU BEAR,
MY GIFT FOR SELF-PROMOTION
IS A TALENT THAT I'LL SHARE.

YOUR TINY LITTLE SEEDLING
CAN BE A MIGHTY TREE,
ALL YOU REALLY NEED TO DO
IS LISTEN MORE TO ME.

YOU CAN HAVE MY EXPERTISE
MY COUNSEL AND DESIGN.
ALL YOU NEED TO GAIN ALL THAT
IS SIGN THE DOTTED LINE.

PEOPLE ON THE VERGE OF A BREAKTHROUGH SEEM TO GIVE OFF A FAINT PERFUME THAT PIGGYBACKERS CAN SMELL A MILE AWAY.

1 Have you ever been weighed down by Piggybackers attaching themselves to your project just at liftoff?

2 Does flattery work when a Piggybacker slings it at you?

3 Are any Piggybackers active in your affairs right now?

4 How can you minimize their impact?

5 Can you distinguish between a Piggybacker and a Booster Rocket, or do you fall for Piggybacker hype?

Excess Baggage: The Art of Choosing Collaborators

Anytime you want to do something that you cannot do alone—when you're switching from a Cessna identity to something bigger, even as big as a jumbo jet, you need to ask the same question all pilots ask: "With that on board, will I be able to get this bird off the ground?"

Some people who show up will arrive with a lot of excess baggage. You don't want those people on your team. They are simply too heavy. You can't fly the plane if you have to keep asking the copilot how she is feeling and if the tone of voice you used to give an order has somehow triggered a flashback to a horrible event or person in her past. No, a copilot should be a copilot; he or she shouldn't walk up the ramp with several suitcases full of lead bars so that every time you

have to tell them something or ask them to do something they have to "process" it. What you want is for them to do it.

Another traveler you don't want flying with you is the fearful flyer. You know the type. The plane is speeding down the runway and you hear these telltale sobs: "This makes me so nervous. I always get like this. Oh, dear God, I think I am going to get sick. Am I hyperventilating? Maybe it's the speed or the height or the guy next to me's tweed suit. . . ." Maybe it's as simple as "No, thanks. Catch a different flight." You can't play pilot *and* Florence Nightingale.

You also want to be careful about skyjackers. They actually want to fly your plane themselves and take it where they want to go. You want your project to be light and sunny

like the South of France. They've got a plan to make it scary and Egyptian. You don't want them. It's a good thing to ask some questions to detect any hidden agendas. If they've got them, you don't want them. You are flying the plane. It's your flight plan. Be clear about that.

What you want are crew members, not yet another dysfunctional family.

1 Have you ever backed away from someone because he or she was simply too heavy to deal with?

2 Have you ever worked with someone who was simply too remote to deal with?

3 Have you ever had a project skyjacked?

4 Who is your favorite creative crew member?

5 What project could you undertake together?

The Language Barrier

Yes, we live in the global village and we're all in the big picture together. On the other hand, you don't want to find yourself speaking plain English to someone who only knows Urdu. In assembling your team, be absolutely certain you can communicate—and clearly and quickly. Here are a few types to watch out for:

Literal Lucy. You know this girl. You say, "I want a great Marilyn Monroe type," and instead of rounding up all the great Marilyn Monroe blondes, she puts out a call for a Marilyn Monroe impersonator with the same bra size, shoe size, and drug problems. You say, "There's something that looks like an asteroid coming toward me," and she wants to discuss it. "What do you mean LIKE an asteroid?" Meanwhile, *splat*. No, you want somebody who understands that "Marilyn Monroe type" means "dishy, come-hither blonde" and "like an asteroid" means "holy shit, help!"

Give-It-To-Me-Again Gus. This is the fellow who is so careful that he doesn't want to make a mistake, even if it kills you. So, when you say, "There's something that looks like an asteroid coming in at two o'clock," he says "Could you repeat that? Was that a.m. or p.m.?" Meanwhile, *splat*.

Second-Guesser Steve. You know this man. He's the one who does what he thinks is best—no matter what you've told him to do. So you say, "North!" and Steve executes "northwest." Then, when you mention this because you almost smashed into a mountain, Steve says, "I heard what you said, Captain, but . . ." Butt out, Steve.

The idea is not to clone yourself but to support yourself. You want to be able to say, "Got it?" and when they say, "Yes," hear the ball hit the glove.

1 Do you have someone in your life who chronically mishears you?

2 Do you have someone in your life *you* chronically mishear?

3 Do you have someone in your life who seems to read your mind, you communicate so perfectly?

4 Do you have someone in your life who helps you say what you mean and mean what you say?

5 Do you have someone in your life who laughs at your jokes and encourages your heart to lighten?

Worrywarts

First of all, you need to know that Worrywarts would like to have a name like Sensible People because that is how they like to present themselves. Their truth is that actually they are Wet Blankets in disguise.

Worrywarts are the people who like to have your doubts for you. They always have a few nagging doubts about why something might not work out and they want to make sure that you've thought of them "for your own good," just so you won't be disappointed.

The Worrywarts are always very careful to tell you that they've got your best interest at heart and they just want to make sure that you've "thought this thing through." Worrywarts are kind of like trolls. They're not really Big Scary Monsters, but they can still really screw things up. The reason is that they are actually carrying a contagious disease called "worry." If you start getting into a conversation with them, you stand a very good chance of catching it. And all of a sudden something that seemed pretty simple, and probably was, starts to seem a little more complicated. When you begin to think something is complicated, you can be pretty sure it will instantly cooperate and get complicated. That's why Worrywarts are off limits.

A really dark way to look at Worrywarts—and sometimes accurate way, if you ask me—is to realize that they get scared when things get fast and zippy and easy. It makes them feel out of control. So they tell you you might be out of control so that you will slow down until they can catch up. They sort of trip you, "accidentally," so that it seems like maybe they were right and you should have been worried after all.

A lot of times agents are Worrywarts. Not always, but a lot. And managers too. Remember, they do like to "manage." But husbands and wives and kids and sisters and brothers and best friends could all be Worrywarts. Shrinks are the biggest Worrywarts of all.

Worry is an addiction. It's something that we do to distract ourselves from what it is we'd like to do. Worry asks "What if I can't?" instead of "How can I?" Worry is what we do so we don't have to do something. Worry is the jitters at the edge of the deep end. Sure, we want to swim, but it just looks so *deep*.

When we are worrying, we are susceptible to the *experts*, not the helpful kind, Real Experts, but the

other kind, Amateur Experts. They are the ones who haven't necessarily done anything but can tell you exactly in great detail why something can't be done by you. They are long on problems and short on solutions. With Real Experts, on the other hand, it's usually a lot simpler. They can tell you in plain English just what to do. That's because even though they are expert, they don't really care about it. They're too busy enjoying what they do. In other words, for Real Experts, "expert" is the by-product, not the identity. The identity is "doer."

Unfortunately, a lot of people seem to be the other kind of expert. You'll know them when you meet them.

1   Who are your Worrywarts?

2   What worries do they carry?

3   What form of worry do you find the most contagious?

4   Who helps you to antidote this form of worry?

5   Have you learned to ask "What can I do?" instead of "What's going to happen to me?" Take one positive action toward your dreams.

Bad Fairies

When you begin to get shiny and bright and look like you just might take off in your career, that's when you start to attract Bad Fairies. These are the people who sidle up to you at openings and say things like "Who do you think you are, Fancy Pants? I knew you when you were nine and you pushed me down on the playground and I've never forgiven you for it and all your bright ideas are never going to get you anywhere and I know . . ." At least, that's their tone.

Pretty much anytime you are having a creative breakthrough you can depend on a visit from a Bad Fairy. I have one who calls me regularly, no matter where I move or how private my phone number is. She hisses things through the phone like "You told me I should try writing ten years ago and now you've abandoned me" or "So-and-so, whom you *might* remember because she retouched a photo of yours twenty years ago, is sick and you might want to call her." (Guilt, guilt, shame, shame!) Bad Fairies always scold and tell you how to be better. They're bitter.

Bad Fairies can be family members or total strangers. They watch your life—not theirs—like TV and they love to tell you when you are doing something they disapprove of. Actually, an attack of Bad Fairies usually means you are on the right track. If you're in a low, lackluster period, they don't bother you much.

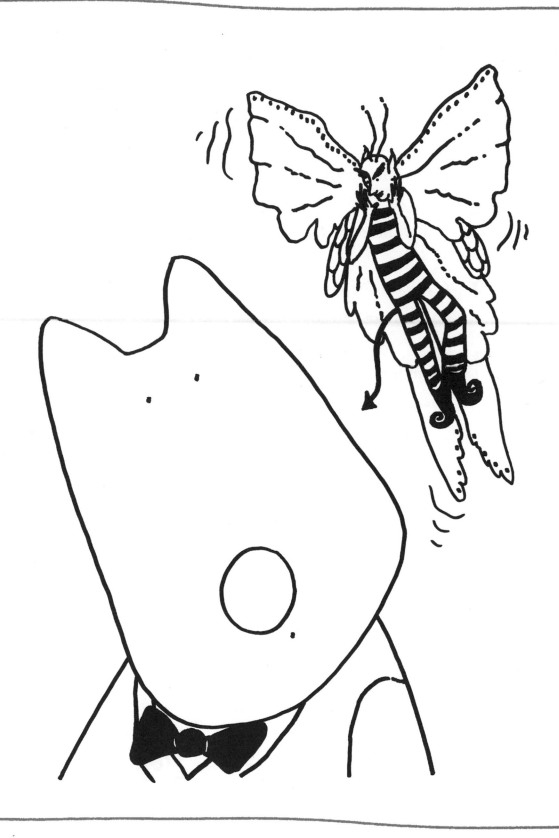

1 Have you ever encountered a Bad Fairy?

2 Is anyone regularly a Bad Fairy?

3 Can you see Bad Fairies clearly, or are you hurt and influenced by what they say?

4 Have you ever tried the Bad Fairy neutralizing trick of writing a poem about the offender?

   "I never tell dreams to my friend, Jerry. He likes to make them sound too scary."

5 Can you think of your Bad Fairy as just a Bad Fairy, like "this dog bites"?

Bad-News Fairies

Another species of nasty stinging pests is what I call the Bad-News Fairies. Bad-News Fairies never like to speak for themselves about their own venom. Bad-News Fairies like to tell you about somebody else's venom. They are the ones who send you your rotten review from Tibet, in case you missed it. They are the ones who drop you a news clipping of your ex-husband and the person he ran off with. They are the ones who "just thought you should know."

Once, when I was acting in a play and still a virgin, a Bad-News Fairy told me that there was a rumor that I had given the boys in the cast syphilis. "I thought you should know what they're saying about you," the Bad-News Fairy told me. (In case I was having any fun.) Do I need to tell you the Bad-News Fairy grew up to work at *The New York Times*, where lots of Bad-News Fairies work?

Bad-News Fairies send e-mail and don't sign it. Bad-News Fairies are officially your friends but they are really your enemies. If you're writing a novel on your lunch hour and they find out about it, you can bet they might tell higher-ups in case you're using company paper or computer space.

Bad-News Fairies are saboteurs. They are motivated by jealousy and competition, but they can't admit it. They've never met their Shadow Side, so they talk about yours to anybody and everybody who will listen. And to you, if you let them.

It's hard to get it together sometimes to say, "Thanks for the good news, you passive-aggressive putz." That's the line that comes later. What I usually do is write a funny little poem about them. This shrinks them very rapidly from the black cloud the size of an A-bomb to a gnat with nasty teeth.

1   Have you ever encountered a Bad–News Fairy?

2   Is anyone a repeat offender?

3   Have you learned to say, "Thanks, but I don't need to know that"?

4   What do you think motivates your Bad–News Fairy? Fear of losing you, or jealousy?

5   Have you ever been a Bad–News Fairy?

Freelance Spiritual Advisers

Although they would never admit it, Freelance Spiritual Advisers are, in fact, a species closely related to Bad Fairies and Bad-News Fairies. They like to present themselves more like hummingbirds than giant mosquitoes but when you get stung by one, you will know the truth. Freelance Spiritual Advisers are in charge of making sure you are serious and pure and haven't sold out. That's their job, and I'm pretty sure Satan gave it to them, although they think God did to judge by their attitudes.

Freelance Spiritual Advisers are always trying to get you to be holier. They act a little like the Church Lady. Let's say you write something really funny. Freelance Spiritual Advisers will wonder if you didn't maybe hurt someone's feelings. (Like they're hurting yours,

but don't mention that.) Freelance Spiritual Advisers are always on the lookout in case you are getting uppity. They want you to be humble and remember your roots, which they will gladly remember for you.

It's like they always want to know "Are you still talking to your mother?" (In my case, the answer is yes and she's dead.) Freelance Spiritual Advisers are usually part of the Pure Art and Real Artists crowd. They like to play the defending saint of the theater or whatever art form you might be having fun in. If you've got a difficult actress in one of your plays, Freelance Spiritual Advisers will tell you she's just being "true to her vision" and maybe tell you to soul-search instead of fire her.

Freelance Spiritual Advisers want to be sure you don't offend anybody.

They just want to be absolutely sure you know how to color inside the lines. (Their lines are much stricter than the Ten Commandments.) If you don't keep the properly pious tone they like, they will worry a little about your spiritual condition. I always want to cast them in a skit about the Virgin Mary as a codependent: "Now, Jesus, darling, don't do that!"

Freelance Spiritual Advisers are the Art-with-the-Capital-A crowd who have their standards written in stone and if you violate them they may just chop those big stone tablets up and throw a few your way. Just say, "Thank you for sharing" and put their name in your icebox. Learn that when anybody starts a sentence "Don't you ever worry?" the right answer is no—even if you do.

1 Have you ever encountered a Freelance Spiritual Adviser?

2 What free spiritual advice were you given?

3 Was it accurate or useful?

4 What spiritual advice would you give yourself?

5 What action could you take on that advice?

Gatekeepers

Ours is a hierarchical society. While we are all created equal, and our Constitution guarantees this, our society actually perpetuates a rigid pecking order, and nowhere is this pecking order more prominent and more toxic than in the arts. A key figure in maintaining toxicity is the Gatekeeper—that person who gives or denies access to higher realms.

Many creative wounds occur at the hands of Gatekeepers who turn aside the gifted aspirant with a cruel, indifferent, or shaming reception. While there is the phenomenon of the good Gatekeeper, it is rare, and we do know it when we meet it. Therefore, it behooves us to identify and demystify the negative Gatekeepers who poison our creative environment. How can you identify a Gatekeeper?

Gatekeepers lack humor. They are very serious and important people—just ask them. Gatekeepers love to lecture. They are fond of dogma and rules. Gatekeepers know how it should be done. They think of themselves as idealists— but very few people measure up to their ideals. Gatekeepers often have a cruel and withholding streak. They are stingy with praise and approval and filled with "doubts"—about *your* value and *your* worth, not their own.

Gatekeepers love the fine print. They are long on problems and short on solutions. Gatekeepers can always tell you more for you to do to live up to their standards. Gatekeepers built the Augean stable. Gatekeepers handed the rock to Sisyphus. If you encounter a Gatekeeper, the task of pleasing them becomes the focus of your life and theirs. At bottom, nothing is

ever good enough for them—especially you and your efforts.

Gatekeepers are frequently found in positions of secondary authority—where they claim to represent the ideals, views, and opinions of those higher up. Very often the ideals, views, and opinions of a Gatekeeper represents are solely their own. Gatekeepers live in the middle—never at the top, and they are certain that you don't. Gatekeepers are not innovators. They play by the rules—the rules you will never measure up to. Gatekeepers like to be scary. They like to use a serious, sanctimonious, and ominous tone. Gatekeepers want to intimidate you. Gatekeepers enjoy shattering self-worth or nudging you off center. A Gatekeeper can't enjoy a good laugh.

Gatekeepers gravitate toward power. If you are powerful yourself, you may attract Gatekeepers of your own. Gatekeepers present a flattering and cajoling face to those they serve, and a very different face to those who knock at the gate. Gatekeepers enjoy the game of catch-22. They thrive on fear. Gatekeepers like to set up a sanctum sanctorum. They require

hushed voices and tiptoes. Gatekeepers are to be found outside the president's door, at the studio gate, in the reception area, and frequently on phone lines. Gatekeepers speak of dire consequences. They read your credit report and murmur, "*Oh*. Oh, dear." Gatekeepers do not know when to make exceptions. They stick to the rules even when the rules are counterproductive.

Gatekeepers like to throw cold water on dreams. They enjoy the aura of power that comes to them from working for the individual or institution whose views they claim to represent. Gatekeepers use phrases like "We here at Bank of Blah-Blah" or "You see, at *this* agency we believe that artists of true merit blah-blah . . ." Gatekeepers undermine the human dignity of those they encounter. They often refuse to crack a smile or make eye contact. Gatekeepers lecture. They say things like "You *see*, in the *theater* . . ."

There are a few important things to remember when dealing with Gatekeepers. First, despite their claims, Gatekeepers do not represent the true personality,

ideals, ideas, or goals of those they claim to represent.

Rule Number Two: Gatekeepers can *always* be evaded eventually. This is what makes Gatekeepers so angry and so crazy. They know they have their finger in the dike and that at any moment some crazy bastard like yourself might punch another hole in the wall they are striving to maintain.

Rule Number Three: Be alert for Gatekeepers. Learn to identify them quickly. Develop a shorthand with a circle of trusted friends that signals "Gatekeeper afoot." If you are alone, weary, and shaky, you are at risk. Vulnerability attracts them. If you have suffered some recent blow, a Gatekeeper will find a way to suggest that somehow your suffering was self-induced, and that if only you were better at—here they introduce whatever doctrine they are representing—then the mishap would not have occurred.

In the world of Gatekeepers, everything is black and white. To be specific, they are white and you are black. They are unsullied by doubts. They live within the lines. A Gatekeeper's life is neat, orderly, and constricted. Viewing the world of human sufferings, Gatekeepers are quick to introduce a note of spiritual Nazism. If you had been more pure, more enlightened, more refined, the "bad" thing would never have happened to you.

Gatekeepers love to fix blame, and the blame lies with you. You are the one who caused everything in your universe. No one else has free will. If you can just be perfect enough, no bad thing will ever happen to you again. How to be perfect? Ask the Gatekeeper. Gatekeepers love committees. Gatekeepers breed with other Gatekeepers. Few things are more frightening than two Gatekeepers engaged in interlocking bureaucracies.

Gatekeepers believe in a frightening god—a god who bears a startling resemblance to a Gatekeeper. Faced with a world of abundant beauty and fantastic diversity, Gatekeepers persist in believing in a god of repression and conformity. The Gatekeeper's god likes you better if you eat brown rice. The Gatekeeper's god speaks to you more clearly if you shut the children out of the room, hush them, and meditate. The Gatekeeper's god is otherworldly— as though this gorgeous paradise beneath our feet were somehow an accident.

Atheists are often brokenhearted believers who mistake the cruelty of Gatekeepers for God's own. How could God allow the Holocaust to happen? A Gatekeeper caused it.

Gatekeepers are passive-aggressive. Seldom overtly hostile, they smile as they deliver the bad news. "Why, I'm *sure* I told you we would need this in triplicate. You *must* be mistaken." Gatekeepers like to have the final word. If you manage to successfully evade them and gain access and approval higher up within the gate, their manner will turn on a dime. "Why, why didn't you *tell* me?" they will say. "Of course if I had *known* . . . " Gatekeepers have two sets of manners, one for the "haves" and one for the "have-nots." Gatekeepers like to keep you a "have-not." They respond to outer cues of your importance. A BMW triggers one set of manners; a Honda Civic invites another.

Gatekeepers believe in rank, rigamarole, and hierarchy. Rather than listen to your insights, they want to know your education, your exact length of sobriety. Gatekeepers are not innovators. They make work for innovators, but they themselves find innovators

threatening until stamped with some outer approval. If you write a novel, a Gatekeeper will want to know if you have an agent and if the manuscript has been published. Gatekeepers always put the cart before the horse. Their question to an artist is not "Do you have talent?" but "Who thinks you have talent?" It works like this:

GATEKEEPER: You're the best actress we've seen for this part. But I'm afraid, since you don't have a name, I can't give it to you.

ACTRESS: How can I get a name if you don't give me a part?

GATEKEEPER: That's not my problem.

ACTRESS: But you see my point.

GATEKEEPER: I'm afraid that without a name we just can't use you.

Gatekeepers require credentials, passports, stamps of approval. Gatekeepers want references. Above all, Gatekeepers want a safety net—a set of variables they can point to should things not work out. "Five people recommended her." "I checked her bank statements from the past three years."

Gatekeepers are sticklers for details, many of which they forget to convey. "But I'm *sure* I told you to bring five passport photos and a copy of your aunt Fannie's birth certificate." "Of *course* your check needed to be certified."

We repeat the encouraging news: Gatekeepers *can* be mollified, cajoled, and evaded. Their persnickety demands *can* be met with humor once we remember the underlying joke which Gatekeepers fail to get: The real creative power lies within each of us, and with God. No Gatekeeper has the power to obstruct, permanently or irrefutably, the flow of anyone's creativity. There is *always* another gate that will swing open.

1 Have you ever let a Gatekeeper discourage you, or have you learned to simply say, "Next"?

2 Have you ever successfully evaded a Gatekeeper? If so, what was your strategem?

3 Have you ever been shamed or intimidated by a Gatekeeper? If so, what was your Achilles' heel?

4 When you meet a negative Gatekeeper, do you strategize or collapse?

5 Is it clear to you that the real power lies in you and with those beyond the gate and not with the Gatekeepers?

The Montagues and the Capulets Game

The way to keep artists from getting things made is to keep telling them they are about to be used and exploited and they should take themselves more seriously. Nonsense. Everybody would get a lot more done if they took everything a little more lightly.

Here's where the Tragedy versus Comedy comes in.

Artists are, by temperament, prone to "Our Gang" thinking. "Let's put on a show in the barn." Management, by temperament, is prone to gang war thinking. "Our Gang versus Their Gang." So, if an artist at Agency A tells his agent or manager he wants to play with someone from Agency B, all hell breaks loose.

"But, they're the Capulets! Are you out of your mind? Sure, you think

you love him, but Romeo, he's CAA, I mean a Montague, and his family is really killers and our family is really wonderful and you don't really love him, do you?" Of course not!

Meanwhile, Romeo is being told "Get a grip. Think about it. This town's full of babes who could play the part. Why are you so stuck on Julia—I mean Juliet. Don't you realize that her family would cut your nuts off?"

We're back to the Telescope Game again, and it's now being played as a contract—oops, contact—sport. "Look here. What did I tell you? Read the tiny print, Juliet! Romeo and his band of thieves are trying to sneak past top billing!"

And over in the Montague camp: "Romeo. Under every skirt's a slipup. Look at this—and here he is handed a microscope, not a

telescope—see that little clause there? She *is* out to get you. Subtle as a deadly microbe is that girl and her crowd."

Sometimes the lovers run off like Tim and Susan did and make movies and babies. Sometimes they get so fed up they jump off cliffs, like Butch and Sundance. Sometimes, like Jeff and Steven and David, they start their own studio. Sometimes they play together anyhow and do it pretty fair.

1 Has anyone ever opposed a creative match you were making?

2 Did this opposition successfully sabotage the project?

3 Have you learned that you have a right to choose your own collaborators?

4 Does anyone in your life consistently oppose your choices?

5 What do they gain by that opposition?

The Twitch, the Flu, the Deadly Disease

When your intent is firm and your flight plan in order, you can expect the arrival of an unwelcome visitor, the Mysterious Malady. Where you were healthy and fear free, you may suddenly have mysterious aches and odd twitches. Weird phobias will rear their heads, dressed in the convincing guise of New Insights and Reality. Let's say you're going to shoot your first short film. Suddenly your eye starts twitching and you have this old fantasy—a phobia, really—that somebody is going to shoot your right eye out. You start seeing snipers crouched on rooftops, except that when you look again they are gone. You develop another pain in your eye and know it will need to be removed. Not the pain, the eye. You wonder if you can shoot with your other eye and maybe wear an eye patch. "I'll just have to," you think. Then your girlfriend says, "Maybe you tore your extended-wear contact. Yes, you have."

Bad head colds, your first ever case of food poisoning, a batch of cluster headaches that make you think "tumor"—these are pretty clear indicators that you are actually going to do what you've set out to do, and your fears know it. Take them as a good sign, sort of like getting shat on by the first robin of spring.

1. Do you suffer dismal or frightening fantasies when you approach your creative jumps? Write them out and place them in a God Jar.

2. Do you suffer irrational but convincing fears of dire outcomes? Write them out and place them in a God Jar.

3. Is your sleep disturbed?

4. Do you endure difficult dreams? Write them out and put them in your God Jar.

5. Do you feel irrationally frightened for those you love? Write a letter, placing them in the hands of a loving God. Put your letter in a God Jar.

6. Post this above your mirror: *These are not premonitions, these are heebie-jeebies. I am allowed to succeed.*

You'll Kill Your Father (or Mother) If You Do That

Certainty that you are about to die is one symptom of impending creative action. Certainty that your parents or loved ones are on the cusp of death is another. "I think it really kills him," we say, "that he never . . ."

We decide that it kills our mother that she's never gone to Paris like she always said she wanted. We think, suddenly, maybe we should send Mom to Paris or Dad to Saudi Arabia, that their dreams are what should come first because if we get ours, it might just kill them.

It's nice to do things for our parents and loved ones. Now is not the time. It will not kill them if you have your dream. They will be right there smiling proudly at Oscar time. Go do your dream. If it all works out really well, then you can help them with theirs.

THEO, SR.

1 Write out your Oscar speech, thanking your parents and your significant other. Put it in your God Jar.

2 Write your parents a list of 25 things you're grateful for. Send it to them.

3 Contact an older mentor figure for the assurance that it's safe and fine for you to achieve success.

4 Pick out the car you'll buy your parents when you're a millionaire.

5 Send your parents a box of Enstrom's Toffee or some fine chocolates.

The Wall

About two-thirds of the way through any creative project, you will run into what I call the Wall. The Wall is a lot like the Sound Barrier. The Wall tells you that you have been a total fool and that you are about to meet with a nasty end.

The reason the Wall is named the Wall is that the best way to deal with it is to remember those old forties prison movies where they stage the breakout. That's how you learn to deal with the Wall.

Here's what I mean. When you first encounter the Wall, you think, Maybe I can break out by scaling that thing, and so you start to do ego sit-ups in your cell. You say, "I am really great (crunch), I am really great (crunch)," and after you've done it about a million times, you

dash for the Wall at midnight and you get about halfway up and the spotlights come on and the voice in the tower says, "Freeze," and there you are, clinging to some skinny rope and hoping they don't shoot you anyhow. No, ego power will not get you over the Wall. It will just get you slammed back into solitary.

The way to deal with the Wall is do what they do in the movies. Don't try to power over it. Surrender that it's too damn tall and go for wriggling under it. Get down on your creative belly and say, "I'm willing to write badly," while you dig with your paws like a terrier. "I'm willing to do this thing badly" will give you the terrier power to burrow under the Wall. You'll end up out and your project might be pretty damn good after all.

1 Write and sign a contract with yourself that says, "I am willing to finish this project even if it turns out bad."

2 Choose one cheerleader friend—carefully. Call him or her and ask for prayers of support.

3 Write out all your fears and resentments connected to this project. Read them to a *very* trusted compatriot, then put them in your God Jar.

4 Pray for the willingness to continue.

5 Continue.

Angels

I don't care what anybody says, angels exist and they sometimes show up to help you get into the air. Sometimes they are dressed like the mechanic. Sometimes they look like just another passenger, until you see the wings sticking out from under their raincoat. Sometimes they don't seem to do anything much except make you feel lighter and that flying is pretty easy.

If you're alert, you will notice your angels when you meet them. Sometimes they open a door for you—"Let me send it to my agent." Sometimes all they do is smile and wink and tell you you are on the right track. Sometimes they just tell you funny stories so that you realize you're in the same club. Sometimes the stories are scary— "Oh, yeah. My wings iced up once over Paramount"—but their point is that they survived them and so will you.

Sometimes your angels will be famous. What do they see in me? you wonder. (The same thing somebody once saw in them.) Sometimes your angels will be so far from famous they might as well be anonymous, but something they say or do will correct your course. Lots of times you won't even know you've been angeled till a long time later.

1   Have you ever encountered a creative angel?

2   Have you ever experienced a mysterious source of creative support?

3   Have you thanked your creative angels?

4   Have you ever been a creative angel?

5   In what area do you need a creative angel?

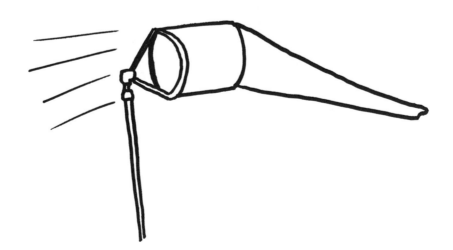

Rocket Fuel

When you are going to fly, you want to make sure that you are putting the right kind of fuel in your tank. There's lots of different kinds of fuel and some of them make engines cough and stall out, so let's look at a few different grades.

First the low test. That's ego fuel. It's when you pump up on *I'm great. I'm great. I'm great. I'm great. I'm great.* That'll get you enough altitude to maybe clear the trees.

Now the next grade. Competition fuel. That's where you fill your tank with I'm-going-to-beat-those-bastards fuel. This gets you sailing about mountain height, but then you look to see how they're doing over at Bamble and Bumble and you crash into a peak. You can tell when brilliant people are using this because they're a little off their game.

Okay, now the high-test. Higher Power Fuel. This is the really leaded stuff that keeps you remembering God is God and CAA is just CAA. This is the stuff that gets you high enough to see other routes over the usual terrain. This is the stuff you want to use, the *God Is My Co-Pilot* stuff. Just try it and see if you don't fly a little more lightly.

1   Do you believe there's "enough" for everyone's dreams?

2   Do you celebrate others' successes?

3   Do you use a spirit of competition as fuel for your endeavors?

4   Have you considered using the spiritual midgets' stratagem of posting a list of your enemies and creating right at them?

5   Have you ever considered using the spiritual giants' technique of praying to be a clean and clear channel for the creative power of the universe to flow through you?

God Is My Copilot

The dangerous thing that happens when you start to get into the Celebrity Zone is that you shoot up and all these False Gods come zooming in close to you, showing their Big Teeth and acting friendly and trying to climb in the window to sit in the copilot seat and play God. Keep the window locked. God is God, He's just quiet about it. These guys just think they are God or wish they were God. They tap on the window to tell you that you are innocent and gullible if you believe in Happy Endings or God and you really need *them*. It's a little like in *Godfather II* when the shop starts going pretty well and the godfather drops by and asks to put his beak in the till.

God is God. Not the godfather. Believe what you believe and keep flying. If one of these characters pastes his face to the window and sneers in a cynical way "I guess you can believe in whatever you want. . . ." Just say, Yes, I can. Say it in your best Clint Eastwood deadpan and keep right on flying.

1 Do you believe God believes in your dreams?

2 Do you believe God supports your dreams?

3 Have you ever had spiritual help with your dreams?

4 Do you ask for spiritual help?

5 When you receive spiritual help, do you call it "coincidence"?

Ground Control

This is a part of your team that it can take a while to find and assemble. Ground Control is the sector that keeps you from panicking when Tokyo Rose is talking in your earphones and your instruments are going blinkety-blink.

Ground Control is, well, grounded. So that if you suddenly decide to head to Venus instead of to Mars, they say calmly, "Check your fuel before you try that, Captain." They do not say, "Boy, what a dumb idea." They *might* say, "Captain, I'm not so sure about that. . . ."

A good agent or manager can be part of Ground Control. So can a really good friend. Ground Control is in charge of alerting you to possible problems, but it is not in charge of inventing them. (When your Ground Control team starts doing that, it will make you ungrounded and furious.) Ground Control has to stay solution-oriented. "I think I can work it out, Captain." Above all, Ground Control needs to remember that you are the captain.

1   What qualities do you look for when you want to be grounded?

2   Whom in your life do you consider grounded?

3   Whom in your life is grounding for you?

4   Whom in your life do you help ground?

5   What do you see as missing or needed to help you feel more grounded?

The Mentor's Good-Bye

You will not be ready for this one—no one is. No one, that is, except your wily mentor, that figure who has given you safety and encouragement and who now, firmly and fiercely, shoves you out of the nest.

"What's this? What are you doing?" you sputter.

"Going to Sukarno," your mentor replies.

"But you're eighty! It's in Asia, isn't it? What are you going to do there?"

"Set up a television network."

With a scenario just like this one, your mentor is suddenly *gone*, vanished, just when you needed him the most, or thought you did. Somehow you thought he'd always be there, guiding you, whispering his directives in your ear.

"You're on your own, kid," he all but said, blinking out like a holograph of Obi-Wan Kenobi, blinking back again to add, "Of course, if you need me, you can always reach me"—he taps his chest—"in here." Then he's *really* gone.

And you're terrified.

"What am I supposed to do now?" you howl. You discover that when you ask, you *do* hear your mentor's voice—"in here."

1   Have you had a mentor?

2   Did you recognize your mentor as such?

3   Have you experienced the mentor's good-bye?

4   Do you still experience your mentor "in here"?

5   Whom do you mentor?

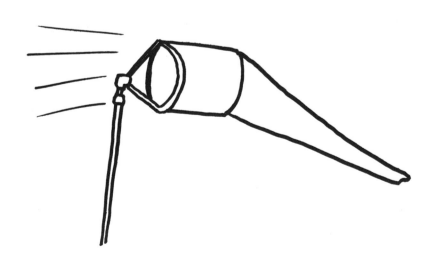

Mikey the Mad Mechanic

Sometimes, as you are taxiing to the runway, you'll meet someone pretty dangerous. I call him Mikey the Mad Mechanic. It goes like this.

You're all checked out. The instruments look good. Your load is the right weight. Everybody is strapped in their seat belts, you are rolling along, when suddenly you spot this guy in a monkey suit, waving wildly. That's Mikey, and you stop because he's a mechanic and he might know something important and besides, he's dead in your path, hopping up and down like the devil on embers and you don't need a murder rap, right? So, you stop.

Mikey the Mad Mechanic is all smiles—concerned smiles a little like those a used-car salesman gets when you are trying to buy the cheaper model car without the fancy options.

"You can't go like this," Mikey says. "Can't you hear that?" (You can't and Leonard Bernstein with a stethoscope couldn't either.) But there is some weird and dangerous something that only Mikey can hear. Before you realize it, he's under there, tinkering and muttering, "Oh, no, oh, no, oh, no," like a bad hooker faking an orgasm. You hear these ghastly little tinkles and tinks as he starts to take apart the engine and suggest new and expensive parts that only he knows how to make. That's right. Mikey is an Expert. Or maybe he's like a snake oil salesman trying to sell you his new potion, the one that cures cancer and works like mental Viagra.

Don't buy it. In fact, don't buy Mikey's whole act. Your old mechanic thought you could fly, and you did too until you met Mad Mikey. He's the nut your engine should be missing.

1   Have you ever encountered Mikey
the Mad Mechanic?

2   What dream did you allow to be dismantled?

3   Does anyone in your life regularly function as
Mikey the Mad Mechanic?

4   What is the payoff for you in taking Mad
Mikey's advice?

5   Have you found a sound sounding board to
replace Mikey's tinkering?

The Desert

No matter where your flight plan is supposed to take you, you will find that in planning your project and getting it off the ground you will inevitably stumble into the alien territory of the desert. This terrain is familiar to saints and mystics, but it's unfamiliar to poor bastards like ourselves. You will know that you are in the desert when people cock their head and look at you funny with something like pity in their eyes. The look says, "I've met a madman. I wonder how long he's been wandering through the wilds." Furthermore, when you describe what you're seeing and where you think you ought to go, no one you talk to will seem to know what you're talking about.

"What do you mean, the second mountain range and the sea of fire? No one can go past there," they will say. Or "What are you talking about? Those things don't exist. They're just myth. You can't really go there."

You can encounter this look when you explain that your company should downsize, or when you say you think your new book should be in a different genre, or when you suggest that painting might be good therapy, or when you decide to start your own press and publish on the Internet. You can stumble into the desert anytime you get a *truly* original idea that doesn't appear on other people's maps.

1   Have you ever encountered the creative desert?

2   Have you ever been warned not to cross it by well-meaning creative elders who have crossed the desert themselves? Did you get their phone numbers?

3   What have you learned to carry with you as spiritual water?

4   Have you learned to repeat the Desert-Crossing Prayer?

    "A step at a time, I am led, guided, and shown safely home."

The Black Gypsy and True North

Put simply, True North is the direction in which we're meant to be heading and the direction we feel good in when we are. Everybody has something marked True North on their inner compass. Everybody can also get their compass spun by the magnetics of other people and their sense of your proper direction.

Just like when you try to shoot the arrow and the Trickster pops out with his fake bull's-eye and tries to get you to aim at that, sometimes you will run into a character I call the Black Gypsy, who will try to convince you that your compass is off and he knows where True North is and you don't. He'll tell you things like your compass is wrong, your map is wrong, and the treasure isn't where you think it is.

The Black Gypsy is a little like a walking Bermuda Triangle. Fly too close to the Black Gypsy's hideout and he'll bring your plane down. He'll even build a city and a landing strip that looks like your own just to fool you.

If you've got a Black Gypsy in your life, you probably know it. You may have bought his map a few times. You may even have a few Black Gypsies. Black Gypsies seem to spring out of the bushes when you are really about to take off.

If you're busy going North (writing a book), the Black Gypsy will tell you you should be going South (building a Web site) or maybe writing a movie. If you've laid a route that goes East (acting class) and then North (acting), the Black Gypsy will tell you to take singing lessons or try modeling and get attention that way. The Black Gypsy always sounds like he's telling you something to help you, but really he just wants a supermodel chanteuse for his Black Gypsy Café.

Another thing the Black Gypsy will do to spin your compass is to tell you that your great idea is either A) bad or B) one that he has a lock on. "I've got a project like that in development right now." (Or "I will when you walk out the door.")

Does this mean you should be paranoid? That everybody is out to get you? No. Absolutely not. It just means the Black Gypsy is only out for himself and you should know that and know him when he crosses your path, and he will.

1   What is True North for you? Name your precise dream.

2   Where would you want to be in relationship to this dream in five years?

3   Where do you want to be in relation to this dream in three years?

4   One year?

5   What action can you take in your current life that begins to move you toward your dream?

Fog

A great way to crash is to run into a little flattery. I mean fog. This is what happens when you listen to people who steam up your glasses about how great you are. Flattery is different from "Nice job, Jake." Flattery is like "Oh, Jake, you're my hero, and you're so brilliant and wonderful and special and, oh, Jake . . ."

Jake, the poor bastard, is like all the rest of us. It's fun to hear this stuff. He forgets it's dangerous. He lets "Oh, Jake" sit in the copilot seat and steam up the *cockpit*. (There's a reason they call it that. The cockpit.)

When the cockpit is all steamed up with "Oh, Jake," it's pretty hard to fly the goddamn plane. Those might be mountains up ahead, or they might be—could they be?—*giant breasts*. Somehow "Oh, Jake" makes breasts seem more likely and then *crash!*

"Jake, you bastard! You hit the goddamn mountain and my tongue almost got caught in your ear. I'm hiking out of here. And don't get your nasty blood on my outfit either, you slime toxin."

People who do "Oh, Jake" to you are filling up your cockpit with fog. They're also filling up your tank with that really low-grade Ego Fuel. When somebody tells you, "Oh, Jake," you can be pretty sure the fog's rolling in and you're about to crash into *Chinatown*.

1 Have you ever had your perceptions fogged by flattery?

2 What errors did you make as a result?

3 Can you distinguish between praise and flattery?

4 Can you praise accurately without flattering?

5 In what areas are you vulnerable to flattery?

Ice

There are a couple of ways to start getting ice on your wings. The first way is that just as you're ready to head down the runway, somebody throws a little cold water on your wings and you start to freeze up with fear.

"Cute little plane, Jake, doubt if it'll make it over the pass. Good luck though." It's easy to see how you can collect a load of ice on your wings from that.

The second way to get it is a little sneakier. You and your hot idea are about to take off and somebody starts icing up your wings with a little pretension and grandiosity. It's sort of like they're spraying a fine mist of "Oh, Jake" on your wings, but when you try to lift off, it weighs a ton. You were trying to write a funny little pamphlet and they tell you it's a Surefire Bestseller and suddenly your little craft is getting pretty heavy.

Nothing ices up the creative wings faster than pretension. You can always tell when somebody has squirted some Oh, Jake Pretension Flattery Number Five into a project. It starts off light and zippy, but by the time it's down the runway, trying to take off, it's a heavily laden jumbo jet carrying everybody's pretentious Nonsense: "The Greatest Movie Ever Made! The Blockbuster Bestseller. Zig, zag, stay on the runway, Jake. Oh, God, try to clear the mountains, Jake, forget about anything fun like loop the loops, just try and land this thing without killing everybody. Jesus, Jake, we all almost died and it's your fault."

So, you want to avoid ice.

1 Is there someone in your life who causes you to freeze up with fear? Take some distance.

2 Is there any aspect of your project that you panic around chronically?

3 How can you get support of that aspect?

4 Locate someone friendly who has successfully accomplished your goal.

5 Take him or her to dinner.

Friendly Fire

You are flying along and it looks like you are going to make it. You are not over enemy territory anymore. You're almost back to home base, you're even talking to them on the way in. "Yeah. I got visual confirmation. I see the Signal Rock. I see the grove of Twisty Pines. . . ." All of a sudden you hear this funny *ffft fft ffft* sound and you don't get it until maybe your left wing catches fire. Friendly Fire! Somebody on your side is mistaking you for the enemy!

Your wife suddenly wants a divorce.

Your kid wants to drop out of high school.

Your shrink thinks you might have unsuspected incest.

Your boss wants to talk about your attitude or your use of company paper to write the novel at lunch hour and how did he find out, oh, yeah? Your friend down there with the antiaircraft gun, the guy who clapped you on the back and walked you to your plane and said he'd make sure you had a great obit if anything happened. He's shooting at you now just as you are on the verge of victory. Why? Why?

Because you are on the verge of victory. Friendly Fire is like a flash flood after a drought, good news of a sort. Fly like a demon straight in and odds are he won't get you.

1 Have you ever been the victim of Friendly Fire?

2 Who was the sniper who attacked you?

3 Are such attacks a regular occurrence?

4 Whom do you call or see to help defend yourself against the devastation of Friendly Fire?

5 Have you ever been guilty of a Friendly Fire attack? What triggered it?

Tokyo Rose

One of the things pilots had to deal with during World War II was a soft, seductive voice called Tokyo Rose. A pilot would be flying and this woman's voice would come on the radio and try to seduce him into doubt about his mission. If a pilot got seduced by Tokyo Rose, the game was over. He went down, turned a traitor on everything he believed, or ended up a POW.

All of us have our run with Tokyo Rose. I call it the Monster in the Ear.

As you can guess, the Monster in the Ear is a lot like the Monster in the Mirror, just the audio version.

1 Who in your life plays Tokyo Rose?

2 Historically, who has played Tokyo Rose?

3 Have you ever betrayed your dream due to negative propaganda?

4 Do you know and identify negative propaganda when you hear it?

5 Have you ever played Tokyo Rose to someone's working dream?

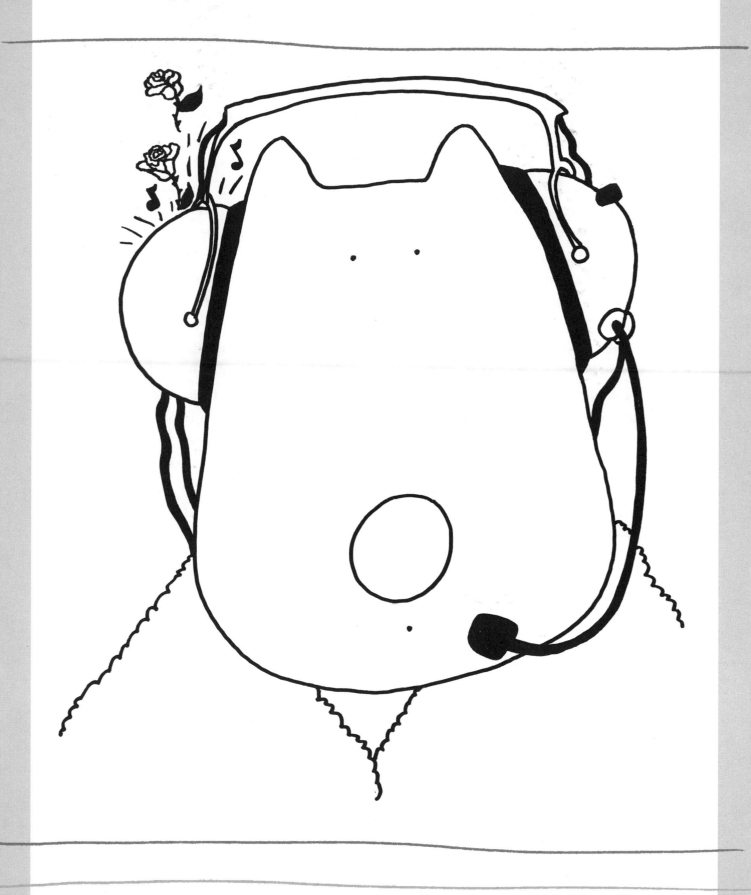

Evade the Radar

This involves the practice of a technique I call Zip the Lip, and it means keep a low profile and don't brag until you are sitting around a campfire *after*. Don't race out and buy a fancy new Hummer. Don't trade up on the house. Don't throw your comfortable clothes away so you're stuck with Armanis a size too small from your Toast and Boast lunches.

Remember: The first rule of magic is containment. Work on the work, not the image. If you are successful, your cheap, shabby offices will mean you are modest. Do not, repeat, do not reach into the Goody Jar and run up an account on the company jet chit. You don't want to show up on the Jealous Schmucks Radar Screen or, for that matter, on the New and Fleeceable Radar Screen. Pet your dog or your wife or your kid's head and practice your Acceptance Speech only in a cold shower.

1   Do you wear your success on your sleeve prematurely?

2   Are you a show boater, talking the talk more than walking the walk?

3   Have you learned to practice this rule: The first law of magic is containment?

4   In what quiet, even secretive, way could you invest in yourself?

5   Whom can you trust to keep your secrets and your dreams?

The Sky Is Not the Limit: The Celebrity Zone

We've got a cultural ceiling on altitude as well as a personal one. When somebody goes sailing past this ceiling and gets too rich or too famous, the Tommy Guns come out. (Usually, critics are shooting them.) There are two variables at work here. Let me try to explain.

When someone is shot into sudden fame, their instruments start spinning wildly. Their Shadow Maker starts racing and everything gets scary. They get disoriented and they worry, rightly, that they might crash. They don't know who to trust. Some of this is because they are seeing big, scary shadows. Part of this is because when somebody gets as bright and shiny as they've just gotten, other people do start acting funny because they are disoriented by all the dazzle too. One reason celebrities act crazy is because they feel crazy, and the other reason is

that other people act crazy around them. Meanwhile, they're supposed to make art.

When somebody gets shot up into what I call the Celebrity Zone, other people look at that altitude and have some pretty funny reactions. Some people look at the altitude and decide the celebrity is a saint with magic powers. They besiege the celebrity with requests or expectations that they should save them (Oprah gets maybe a million requests like this a week and so did Madonna for a while). When the celebrity doesn't act like a saint and save them—which is something they could try doing themselves— then these people get very mad. That's how we get snipers and stalkers.

Another thing that happens when people fly into the Celebrity Zone is that to some other people if they

are that Big and up there, they must be Mommy and Daddy. These people want their celebrities to act responsibly and do what they think they should do. This is why we get tabloid articles scolding celebrities for overspending, overscrewing, overdoing.

For still other people when somebody gets shot into the Celebrity Zone—and this happens a lot when a moviemaker goes there—the people left behind identify with them, cheering them on, but are scared of being abandoned. So, they start acting like the celebrity is always betraying his or her "roots." For artists this means that new directions are seen as betrayals by most critics, who are jealous little brothers and do not want their Our Gang—Marty and me or Steven and me or Francis and me—fantasy shattered.

Critics act a lot like pissed-off younger brothers. They feel betrayed when an artist does what's up next for him or her instead of what little brother wants done. No matter how good the new work is, they say it's rotten. They scold the artist for switching genres like they are cheating in the game they have set up. Male artists get this a lot.

And sometimes the new work isn't good—yet. It's hard to go in a new direction when everyone is screaming at you to swim the way they want you to. Trying to make a movie or album is always hard, but trying to do it with people wanting something else is like trying to finish a marathon with people on the curb all yelling, "You'll never make it!"

Remember, too, that when somebody gets shot into the Celebrity Zone, their instruments go crazy and a lot of people start suddenly "managing" their career. Their own perfectly good instincts get number one confused and number two invalidated. The team members they had to help them get so far are suddenly removed. "This time we want you to use a veteran," and the artist is apt to get overrun by Experts. Old friends get pissed off being asked to be conduits to the New Star and they back off too. The Big Cheese stands alone, and it's miserable.

If this is bad on the men, it is hell on the women. They get so much "save me" and "be the Madonna" projected on them that they can go a little crazy. We watched Madonna play out both Madonna and whore, which gave her a little more latitude. As an artist she danced with the projections she received, but most women get stuck with the projection they happen to look or sound like.

How you got famous also helps determine what projection you get stuck with. When Bill Clinton got the presidency, he was suddenly supposed to fit the Good Daddy archetype. When Hillary Clinton got famous, she went through first Good Mommy (Madonna) and then whore. When a celebrity doesn't fit or doesn't want the projection they've been cast in, they get punished for deviating from it. Oprah is supposed to be Earth Mother powerhouse sob sister; she gets punished whenever she tries acting or getting too thin or glamorous. Oprah is supposed to be nice and soulful, period. All her new formats and forays into film are her attempt to say her own name, not just take her projection.

For celebrities, the projection they are stuck with works like "Me and My Shadow." It's always there, tagging along, botching up new perceptions. Although I'd been an artist for two decades, when I published *The Artist's Way*, people

forgot that and projected "Teacher" or "Spiritual Fairy Godmother" on me. I had lots of people tell me I was "just like" the Good Witch from *The Wizard of Oz*. Did she write for *Rolling Stone* or *Miami Vice*? When I published a crime novel, critics were like "What is a New-Age guru [their description] doing writing a mystery?"

One woman asked me if she touched my skirt would she be able to write her novel. I said, "No, but you might want to try using the tools." I call this the Magic Wand School of Spiritual Growth and Development.

And so, to continue, when celebrities reject their projection, the public can get angry. (Certainly critics do, because it wrecks their artist-should-do-what-I-say game.) No wonder the Celebrity Zone is such a scary space. No wonder celebrities clump together. It's not just snobbery and Aren't We Groovy? It's having other people to talk to about the craziness. Most people have no idea how scary it is to have weird people with funny-looking eyes show up on your doorstep, convinced you are their destined mate. Most people have no idea the psychic toll it takes to get bags of mail begging for help when you feel pretty tapped out yourself. Most people don't get charged four times the going rate. That's why celebrities flock together. For emotional safety.

Fame is a spiritual drug—grass and coke, to be specific. The high-adrenaline, I-will-eat-you-for-lunch aspect of fame is the coke. The compass spinning, room spinning, am-I-nuts-or-is-it-you-or-are-both-of-us? aspect is the grass. Just watch some poor bastard try to survive the week 20 million people watched him on TV or how she sounded stupid in front of the whole world on the Oscars and forgot to thank her mother. Come to think of it, the real drug may be acid.

Instead of thinking "Celebrities are such jerks," we might try practicing the thought, Maybe fame's that hard to handle and I'd act like a jerk a little too. After all, the Celebrity Zone bears a close resemblance to the Twilight Zone. (You wore braces and glasses and couldn't get a date in high school and now you get letters asking for your old panties. Yes, it's weird.)

1 Who in the Celebrity Zone have you ever judged or ridiculed?

2 Who in the Celebrity Zone handles themselves with grace?

3 Who is a role model for you in dealing with the craziness of the Celebrity Zone?

4 What landmark would indicate to you that you had entered the Celebrity Zone?

5 What behavior do you swear you will *never* indulge in?

The Chorus of Woes

The truth is that making things is fun, but you are never supposed to say that. What you are supposed to do is remember the lyrics to "We Are Swell but Life Is Hell." That's the song where the chorus goes, "Life is no travelogue. Life is all dog eat dog . . ." You know the song. The volume on it gets cranked up whenever things get zippy. It has that one verse,—

"Remember the odds and the angry gods"—that they love to play in the elevator on your way to creative meetings.

In Greek tragedy, the chorus was supposed to warn the hero. This is not tragedy. You are not being warned. You are being scared and scolded for acting like you've got a head on your shoulders. You do. Use it to wear earplugs.

REMOVE BEFORE FLIGHT

1 List the pettiest and most hilarious negative complaint you've heard recently. ("Yeah, my damn Jaguar, it's almost more trouble to keep up than my damn Mercedes.")

2 Write an elaborate complaint about something you actually love.

3 Nominate someone for an Oscar in griping.

4 Watch a catastrophe/calamity movie. *They've* got something to complain about.

5 Pick your next project and start griping now. Gripe on the page for five minutes. Then spend five more minutes converting your negative gripes to positives. "I'm so confused" becomes "I'm getting clearer by the minute."

The Tragedy Club

Once you start to make it big, they want to invite you into the secret clubhouse—all of them. If you go, you find that a lot of times they've gotten used to sitting in the comfy clubhouse chairs, talking, so they don't fly very much anymore. They talk about flying.

How hard it is. How you can't fly like you used to. The tragic spiraling costs. The terrible, terrible odds. They tell each other Cautionary Tales so nobody goes off half cocked and leaves the clubhouse to try flying again. If you sit in the clubhouse long enough, eating enough gooeys and enjoying enough goodies, you'll start dozing in your chair, sometimes for years.

Wake up.

1 Write a tragic/comic monologue of the worst stories you have ever heard related to someone trying to do your projects.

2 Pick a negative role model and write about *exactly* what bothers you in his or her behavior.

3 List five major kvetchers in your acquaintance.

4 Choose a positive role model and write about *precisely* what attracts you to his or her personal style.

5 Drop a call of encouragement to someone behind you on the trail.

The Goodies

One of the ways artists are controlled is by doping them up on the Goodies. Artists get addicted to Goodies the way we used to get addicted to everything else. Jets! Fancy offices! Acres of Armani! Now we've got 12-step programs for everything else but what we really need—a 12-step program for the Goodies.

We need to be able to sit around in dirty basements and say, "I almost slipped. They told me that if I made this godawful technowarpcrash film I could get to use the jet. The jet! My mouth started to water. I couldn't remember anymore why I might have wanted to make the good little movie. I almost went for it." And people would cluck sympathetically.

People everywhere have their own version of the jet. Artists at all levels are being bribed off their paths all the time.

1 The Buddhists call Goodies "attachments." Make three columns. In column 1, list five goodies you could grow attached to. In column 2, list the emotional or intellectual quality the Goodie symbolizes for you. In column 3, list an action you could take to embody that quality for yourself.

Before, During, and After Friends

Success brings with it many new opportunities and acquaintances. These can be heady and exhilarating. So heady and so exhilarating that we can lose our bearings. This is where the little brownie song should be sung by one and all as we ascend the stairway to stardom:

Make new friends, but keep the old
One is silver and the other gold. . . .

Before, during, and after friends are those who love us not only for what we have become but also for what we have been. They may be your aunt Bernice, Dan whom you went to St. Joseph's Grade School with, Rosemary who was your party playmate the summer after college. They may be your spouse and your children. They could be your high school English teacher and the guy you lifeguarded with summers on the Cape. These are your oldies but goldies and they may include a few pets. Your golden Lab loved you before your National Book Award and views all your phone interviews as competition to the more important business of Going for a Walk. Remembering to go for a walk, particularly with a before, during, and after friend, can go a long, long way toward making success worth having. It's lonely at the top if you have jettisoned your friends along the way.

1   Select five people whom you consider to be your before, during, and after friends. Go to the five-and-dime and buy five whimsical tokens of your affection and friendship and shared interests. Mail these to those friends.

Your Baggy Corduroys and That Awful Sweater

Just because you can now afford to doesn't mean you should trade in all of your comfort clothes for some snazzy Armanis you are afraid to eat pasta in. Old clothes are old friends. They give us a sense of continuity and comfort. The ratty bathrobe you wrote your novel in deserves a place of honor. The sweatshirt you sweated out your twenties in can keep you connected to that younger self. Realized dreams are sweeter if we remember the days when they were only dreams. The baggy pajamas you wore writing your children's book can make the child in you a little more comfortable when success seems too grown-up and scary. Your track team T-shirt might mean more to you than a closet full of Hugo Boss. You be the boss and decide.

1 Survey your wardrobe for oldies but goldies. Mend any tatters. You may wish to replace missing buttons or add decorative touches, like annoying little jingle bells. These clothes should make you feel both coddled and cuddled. Defend them against any and all who wish to "spiff you up."

About Those Socks

There are lots of ways to celebrate, and most of them are a terrible idea. Flying with that blonde to Paris can max out your credit card and your credibility. The new BMW will need to be washed more often than your old beater. The magnum of champagne will go to your head and your pocket. You might want to try red socks.

There is something about a good pair of bright red socks that says, "Yep, I like myself. I like life. I'll probably like you and you'll probably like me." Red socks are a great way to celebrate. It's hard to be depressed, alienated, and serious in a pair of snappy red socks. It's hard to be self-important and cranky. God probably wears red socks.

1   Buy five pairs of fiery red socks. A variety is recommended—crew socks, knee socks, anklets, sweat socks—and for the ladies, fire-engine-red tights if you can find them. If you are domestically inclined, you may wish to knit your own. Many plot lines have been improved in the process.

Flight Procedure

Keep a Flight Log

Three pages of longhand morning writing each day keeps your trajectory clear. As you record distractions, obstacles, moods, breakthroughs, and the simple business of getting there, you also identify allies, Piggybackers, and unforeseen sources of support and supply. Think of this flight log as an indispensable adviser, the trail of bread crumbs into the creative forest and back out again.

Fill the Tank

At least once a week, for at least an hour, take the time to refill your creative fuel tank by doing something solitary and festive. Be alert for the ideas and insights that come swimming to the surface

during this set period of receptivity. Remember that art is an image-using system and that you must take the time to replenish your image supply if you are to have sufficient creative juice to complete your flight.

Landmarks

Flying east to west in America, you cross the Appalachians, the Mississippi, the Rockies—all landmarks that tell you of your progress. On your creative journey, be alert to note and celebrate your landmarks: first draft done, made it into a juried show, found an agent, published an excerpt, made the new and noteworthy column, etc. By logging your landmarks into your flight log, you gain an accurate perspective on progress gained and territory left to travel.

Walk on It

A good twenty-minute walk moves you into the Imagic-nation, where dreams are clarified and capitalized. Frequent walks keep your creative metabolism moving and allow you to access higher frequencies of inspiration.